MAD
HUNGRY
FAMILY

MAD HUNGRY FAMILY

120 ESSENTIAL RECIPES TO FEED THE WHOLE CREW

Lucinda Scala Quinn

Photographs by Jonathan Lovekin

ARTISAN

NEW YORK

Library of Congress Cataloging-in-Publication Data

Scala Quinn, Lucinda.
Title: Mad hungry family / Lucinda Scala Quinn.
Description: New York : Artisan, a division of Workman
Publishing Company, Inc., [2015] | Includes index.
Identifiers: LCCN 2015037712 | ISBN 9781579656645
Subjects: LCSH: Cooking. | LCGFT: Cookbooks.
Classification: LCC TX714 .S3153 2015 | DDC 641.5—
dc23 LC record available at http://lccn.loc
.gov/2015037712

ISBN 978-1-57965-664-5

Design adapted from Jennifer S. Muller and Nick Caruso

Artisan books are available at special discounts when purchased
in bulk for premiums and sales promotions as well as for fund-
raising or educational use. Special editions or book excerpts also
can be created to specification. For details, contact the Special
Sales Director at the address below, or send an e-mail
to specialmarkets@workman.com.

Published by Artisan
A division of Workman Publishing Co., Inc.
225 Varick Street
New York, NY 10014-4381
artisanbooks.com

Published simultaneously in Canada by
Thomas Allen & Son, Limited.

Printed in Malaysia

First printing, August 2016

1 3 5 7 9 10 8 6 4 2

CONTENTS

PREFACE: THE TRILOGY

Reflections are dubious and often inaccurate, so thankfully some version of this mom's life has been told in recipes.

Some people scoffed when *Mad Hungry: Feeding Men & Boys*—a cookbook of recipes, strategies, and survival techniques for bringing back the family meal—was published in 2009. "What about girls?" they said. I'm the only sister of three brothers and mother to a trio of sons. All I knew about the general eating habits of girl children was that they rarely asked for thirds, did not want another meal as dinner was being cleared from the table, and—most mind-bendingly—would tolerate any crappy old salad put in front of them because girls were *supposed* to eat salads. No, that first book was a chronicle of nurturing young boys into existence, and feeding their emerging appetites with simple and satisfying foods. It's an edible roadmap for the first leg of the journey, which turned out to be the easiest part. Once my husband and I had our third son, life went crazy. If not for the anchor of mealtime, the thin chord that held our sanity and survival together might have snapped completely.

My next family cookbook, *Mad Hungry Cravings,* was a cry to my guys during their most vulnerable teenage years: Please stay connected to me! In it, I promised to cook at home the foods they craved in the outside world. They were New York City kids, and every single day, I prayed for their safe return to our apartment. They'd begun to let go, just as planned, and although they were learning to be *in* the world, they weren't quite ready to inhabit it independently. Until they figured that out, I had food cooked and a table for them and their friends to gather around. I was hoping to save them from their hormone-fogged selves for one more meal.

Much of the time this plan actually worked. It involved cooking lots of faux-Chinese takeout; deli-style bacon, egg, and cheese sandwiches; imitation fast-food fried chicken; hot dog–cart hot dogs; burger-shack burgers; large bowls of pasta; and homemade potato skin/chicken wing–type foods. And, of course, there were always a couple of vegetables offered, too. I wanted them to recognize cooking as an expression of love—something worth coming home for. At times, that seemed like a foreign concept, especially during those moments when they acted like they hated me. But inside, they just wanted to eat.

This book completes my trilogy. I've hooked my sons, our friends, and many strangers on the merits of home-cooked meals, and these pages reveal the method to my madness—with the essential recipes and the often unexplained little tips that will lead you, your children, and even the most stove-adverse to success in the kitchen.

OPPOSITE: Jerk Chicken and Mango Chutney Sandwiches (page 46)

A MOTHER'S STORY

When my oldest son, Calder, smells garlic cooking in oil or butter, he thinks of home. And when he smells garlic burning in butter or oil, he thinks of how—to use his words—I was "always harping about *never* doing that." One by one, these recollections are strung together in childhood without us even knowing it—like a strand of pearls of priceless value. All of us have them.

If someone had told me thirty years ago at my shotgun wedding that my cooking would give my son a sense of comfort, that he would learn from me this most important life skill of feeding himself, I would have saved myself so much worry—there are so many things no one tells you about being a mom! Like, your heart will never again be unburdened in this lifetime. Like, in the lust for young babies—for that sweet baby-musk smell, the warmth, the lightness—is lost the reality that someday those infants will grow into defiantly independent young men who walk this earth wearing your last name and possessing a will you can no longer alter. I had an inkling that no one might exasperate me more in my whole life, but I was surprised to discover the possibility of raising some of the best friends I'll ever have.

When Calder was born back in the 1980s, no one was telling me any of this. It was an era of shoulder pads and power careers for women my age—and I opted out of both. When I was a young mother, it was totally uncool to be in the kitchen cooking for your family. (Hadn't the whole point of the sexual revolution been to take a pass on cooking or kids—and preferably both?) When I was asked, "What do you do?" at dinner parties in New York City, nothing stopped the conversation like answering, "Cooking food and raising my kids." Surely, that's what takeout and nannies were for! Nourishing my kids

came naturally to me, so I chose that over working outside the home, for a while anyway. And yes, we were almost always broke: when I took the boys on our regular outing of hitting every playground along Central Park West between 110th Street and Columbus Circle, I brought along plenty of home-popped popcorn and water—there were no luxuries like $1 hot dogs or pretzels from the street vendors. Lots of nights, as we waited for the next meager paycheck to turn up, we were fortified by Black Beans and Rice (page 138).

Now, when I think back on it, it's ironic that barely making any money set me up beautifully for what would become—when my youngest was seven—the next phase of my career. When our family was young, home cooking nourished our boys into this world. It nurtured and educated them, too—my home kitchen is too small and too crowded for them *not* to pick up the skills (and the smell of garlic) needed to cook. Being able to cook is an expression of independence, a clear execution of self-reliance. Even so, food will always be our connector, the lingua franca we learned together. When the boys were going through their difficult adolescence (miserably timed to coincide with my difficult perimenopause—*another* tidbit no one bothered to tell me!), this food language was our one reliable connection. Now, our boy-men, set free to roam this life, at least have that kitchen rhythm to cling to. These twentysomethings will still eat a meal with us, prepare a meal with us, be taken out for a meal, and most important of all, cook for themselves and others—their mother included.

I still worry that they will turn out all right, find their own ways, survive their own mistakes (and mine, for God's sake!). Worry whips up when least expected, and then swallows unhealthy amounts of time. But just as quickly as lightning strikes, the sun peers out of the clouds—one of my sons cooks me a plate of the carbonara from their childhood, and my mind is again at ease.

OPPOSITE: *Carbonara* (page 122)

IX

THIS I PROMISE

The best way to cook is to give yourself no choice but to buckle down and actually do it, for whatever reason is the most consistently motivating— be it saving money, eating healthfully, or just feeding a family that's hungry multiple times each day. At first it will feel difficult. It might leave you sore. You will be shocked when, a couple of hours after finishing lunch, someone has the temerity to ask you what's for dinner.

Committing to cooking may feel like an assault of inconvenience at times (not to name names, but hey, Monday night: almost everyone hates you and wishes you were never born). But slowly you will get into the rhythm of preparing these meals and mastering essential skills, such as shopping for groceries and stocking a refrigerator and pantry, until arriving home from work just a short time before dinner will no longer feel like a losing battle. You will find pleasure in having ingredients on hand that let you pull together a meal that tastes really good and makes your people happy. Once you get in the habit, you'll always buy two or three cans of plum tomatoes and black or white beans. Your pasta selection will rival that of the neighborhood Italian restaurant, and you'll never be without onions and potatoes—and maybe even shallots! Jarred spices and herbs will get good workouts, and you'll be able to gauge which you should buy and when. The fridge will be stocked with bottled condiments (such as sesame oil and Dijon mustard) that actually get used up in less than a year. Better yet, you will find yourself enjoying the process— and you'll discover the inspiration and confidence to improvise and get creative.

Think of it as cooking like a boss—the leader who's in charge. That's you! Consider professional chefs, the bosses of restaurants: they get to walk in and do the fun part because they have prep cooks, dishwashers, and a few meals off. To cook like a boss daily, you have to prep and act as sous-chef (and clean dishes) for yourself—or rope in other family members! At first this will seem overwhelming, but once you learn to grab time where you can find it (like a Sunday afternoon chopping fest, or a greens-cleaning convention), you'll pick up some essential skills that will make cooking meals a lot easier. For example, you might have the foresight to roast two chickens, and then shred one for later in the week because you know your family will want tacos or sandwiches. Then you, too, will have the option of just walking in and doing the fun part—creating great flavors and satisfying meals from things in the kitchen.

As for hard-core skills, they will come. All you really need is the willingness and the discipline to carve out some time each week (and/or day) to shop, chop, and roll. Follow the recipes I have chosen for these pages, which I consider road maps. Once you've cooked them a time or two, you will find ways to tailor them to suit your family's particular tastes and needs. You know where you are and you know where you want to go; the recipe shows you the route. After you follow the path a few times, it will become second nature. Let this book be the "Attaboy!" (or "Attagirl!") that helps you figure it out.

Believe in the Power of Home Cooking

The ordinary act of preparing food to nourish yourself and others just might be one of the single greatest gifts you can share with a fellow human being. The beautiful quotidian of serving something like Spaghetti and Simple Tomato Sauce (page 120), and what that does for the soul of your family, is priceless. If you cook for the people you love and teach them to cook for themselves, they will pass it on.

Bring Confidence to the Kitchen

Fiercely embrace those mealtime moments that come around and around and around—like clockwork—day in and day out. Such awareness makes the best of a necessary situation so that when you prepare breakfast or dinner, you can actually learn to enjoy the process rather than feeling enslaved by it. It becomes a lens through which you understand the world. With the will to participate, and a little experience, mealtime becomes an anchoring cadence for your day instead of one that can overwhelm.

Don't Worry About the Joneses

Forget any preconceived notions you have about what it takes to cook. All you need is a small workspace, a cutting board, a good knife, a utility spoon, one good pot, and a heat source. Don't rush out to buy a twelve-piece knife set. Choose your tools and workspace to suit you. Do you want to do all your cutting jobs with a paring knife? Don't be afraid to make that your go-to knife! If you have no choice in the matter, either for economic or space reasons, remember that the best food comes out of some of the humblest kitchens. Still, should the kitchen goddess rain resources down on you—go for the coolest, most badass rig you can imagine!

Buy Real Food and Cook It Well

The only imperative is to buy real food in its natural state—be it beans and rice or steak and potatoes—and to cook it well. Food that tastes good will deeply satisfy you and the people you cook for. All it takes is a little effort, practice, and the know-how contained within these pages. In no time—if not already—you and your family will be reaping the plentiful rewards of home cooking.

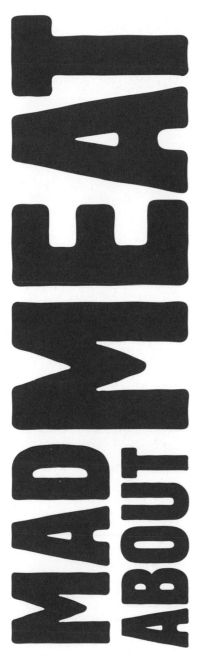

MAD ABOUT MEAT

OPPOSITE: Thai Red Ribs (page 10)

PORK HAS FLAVOR-SWAGGER

A text popped up just now on my phone from my son Luca, who's away at college. It's a Saturday afternoon in Indian summer October.

HIM: mom I really want to start looking for jobs for the summer

ME: where are you?

HIM: I'm actually in Woodstock, New York with Nick and Erin, Nicks girlfriend

HIM: I also brought a pork shoulder

A pork shoulder went from Albany to Woodstock in his knapsack on a Bonanza bus? And so, in an instant, our talk turned from discussing the vague and terrifyingly vast future to the comfortingly immediate plan: pork for dinner, cooked with friends. If you're wondering how a college kid with no car, no true kitchen, and a limited budget ends up with a 7-pound bone-in pork roast, I can only answer: the boy is his mother's son. Once a week I served pork chops, and weekends often meant some sort of slow-roast pork shoulder or carnitas (a crispy pork filling for tacos).

Because I was regularly feeding five people every night, I made a habit of buying a bone-in pork roast every week for 69 cents a pound at the local grocery. We could make a big family (and often last-minute friends) feast one night and use the bone for a beautifully flavored bean meal the next day.

But talking about home economics undersells this meat's appeal. Simply put, pork has swagger. It has all the right components for success—savory, fatty, juicy, crispy, over-the-top wow factor. Throw down any recipe, flavoring, or technique, and—once you learn how to cook it—pork will deliver the goods every time.

As I texted with Luca, I admit I might have been a little too ambitious right off the blocks. I might have flooded his poor iPhone with text-by-text instructions for a complex caramelized orange pork, and that daunted him. But as he questioned me, the real truth behind the recipe came out.

HIM: ok gotta see if I can collect all those items here. If not I really wanna go to the grocery store to get them, just like soy sauce and sweet wine

ME: also you can swap the stuff that nails the particular flavor or texture of an ingredient

HIM: so it takes a total of 8 hours to make?

ME: how big is the meat and does it have a bone?

HIM: yes it does. It's a 7-pound shoulder

ME: then yes the recipe is the correct time to dankness

HIM: damn is there any way to expedite the marinating process?

ME: yeah just do what you can do. Poke the meat all over so it can soak in. It'll flavor up while cooking

HIM: so how much time can I shave off the marinade?

ME: pretty much all but don't scrimp on cooking time

HIM: ok yeah I won't

And this seemingly throwaway conversation flipped a switch in my approach to the recipes in this book (beginning with the recipe for this very dish, which follows). With my son's voice in my head, I've made sure to encourage lots of shortcuts, give permission to swap ingredients, and call attention to the subtle details between the lines in a recipe that we recipe writer–cooks take for granted. While his summer job uncertainty still loomed, the bubbling, caramelized, citrusy, salty pork shoulder would be his dinner tonight.

caramelized orange pork roast

serves 10 to 12

This pork roast marinates and cooks in the same delicious sauce for 5 hours—low and slow in the oven—but don't be turned off by the long cooking time. It needs no babysitting, so you can use this time to do other chores in the house while it's cooking and filling your nose with its intoxicating and mouthwatering aroma. It's essential not to undercook the roast, but overcooking it is practically impossible. On the advice of my new-to-cooking son, I've included several options for ingredients so you can use the ones you have on hand (see page 6).

1 cup white wine

1 cup soy sauce

¾ cup brown sugar

½ cup Sriracha hot sauce

⅓ cup whole-grain mustard

¼ cup rice wine vinegar

Finely grated zest and juice of 1 orange

6 garlic cloves, minced

One 6- to 8-pound bone-in pork shoulder (if skin-on, score in a crosshatch pattern)

1. Whisk together all the ingredients except the pork in a large roasting pan. Poke the pork all over with the tip of a sharp knife or a fork, to allow the marinade to penetrate, and place in the pan with the marinade. Turn the meat several times while it marinates in the refrigerator for at least 4 hours. If you don't have 4 hours, do it for as much time as you have. Overnight is good, too.

2. Preheat the oven to 325°F. Loosely tent the roasting pan with foil, and cook the marinated pork for 1 hour per pound. Every hour, drizzle the meat with the pan sauce, and add ½ cup water as needed to prevent the sauce from becoming too concentrated and scorching in the pan.

3. Remove the foil. If the pork is caramelized at this point, continue cooking at 325°F; if not, raise the heat to 375°F. Cook until an instant-read thermometer reads 190°F (the point at which the cartilage melts), about 1 hour more, basting the pork with the pan sauce a few more times. Continue to add water as needed.

4. Remove the roast from the oven. Let rest for 20 minutes, loosely tented with foil. Shred or slice the meat and return it to the pan with the sauce. Serve with extra sauce spooned over top, along with rice and a green such as Garlicky Collard Greens (page 162).

INGREDIENT SUBSTITUTIONS

Sometimes you don't have the exact ingredient called for in a recipe, and that's okay! There are plenty of items in your kitchen that will play the same role as the one called for.

Almost every marinade, sauce, or, indeed, any memorably tasty dish is a blend of six components: **heat, acid, liquid, sweet, salt,** and **spice.** While lots of recipes call for very specific versions of each, have the confidence to substitute according to taste . . . or pantry supplies. Using the Caramelized Orange Pork Roast on the previous page as an example, consider these alternates:

HEAT • **Sriracha hot sauce:** any spicy red chili sauce or 2 tablespoons crushed red pepper flakes

ACID • **Rice wine vinegar:** any vinegar (if you chose a tangy variety, just use a little less, as rice wine vinegar has a milder flavor than most vinegars), or lemon or lime juice

LIQUID • **White wine:** use any wine you have on hand, or vermouth, beer, mirin, or broth (something with a little aroma)

SWEET • **Brown sugar:** regular sugar, molasses, maple syrup, or honey

SALT • **Soy sauce:** fish sauce or Worcestershire sauce (something salty and savory)

SPICE • **Whole-grain mustard:** Dijon mustard, stone-ground honey mustard, brown mustard, Coleman's dry mustard (cut the amount by half, as dry mustard is stronger than others), or bright yellow hot dog mustard (it brings an earthy-tangy flavor)

OPPOSITE: Pork Roast with Garlicky Collard Greens (page 162)

green pork chili

serves 8 to 10

This chili is a revelation—spicy and deeply wholesome, with an unmatched yin-yang combination of herbaceous peppers and soft, savory meat. A large bone-in pork shoulder (or butt or picnic ham) remains a total bargain for feeding a group. Ask the butcher to remove the bone and cube the meat, or do it yourself: Use a thin, sharp knife to slice along the sides of the bone. Remove the bone and reserve it for another recipe, or make some broth to use as the liquid for this recipe (see below). Remove the layer of skin and fat and cut the pork into cubes.

4 pounds boned pork shoulder, cut into 1½-inch cubes (bone reserved)

Coarse salt

2 tablespoons vegetable oil

3 large onions (preferably white), chopped

1 whole head garlic, peeled and minced

12 green chilies (such as Hatch, Anaheim, or poblano), roasted, peeled (optional), seeded and chopped into 1-inch squares

6 cups chicken or pork broth (see below)

10 flour tortillas, warmed

1 Heat a large Dutch oven or other heavy-bottomed pot over medium-high heat. Coat the meat with a generous amount of salt. Swirl the oil into the pot. When it shimmers, work in batches to brown the meat on all sides, 6 to 8 minutes per batch.

2 Transfer the browned meat to a plate. Remove excess fat from the pot, leaving behind about 2 tablespoons. Add the onions and garlic to the pot. Sauté until softened, about 3 minutes, scraping up the browned bits on the bottom of the pan. Add the chilies, stir to combine, and cook until softened, about 5 minutes more.

3 Return the meat to the pot and pour in the broth. Add 2 teaspoons salt. Bring to a boil, then partially cover, reduce the heat, and simmer, stirring occasionally, until the pork is almost tender, about 1½ hours. Remove the lid and continue to simmer until the liquid has thickened a little and the meat is tender, about 1 hour more. Season with salt to taste and serve with warm flour tortillas.

RESERVE THAT PORK BONE

To make an enriching broth that can be used in place of chicken broth in any pork dish: Place a pork bone in a large pot with 1 tablespoon vinegar and water to cover. Bring to a boil and skim off all the foam that rises to the surface. Add a few peppercorns and simmer for 2 hours. Strain the broth and return it to the heat until reduced by half, about 30 minutes. Salt to taste.

ABOUT HATCH CHILIES

Hatch chilies are truly one of America's best regional and seasonal treats. These long, narrow, light-green guys are grown in the New Mexican valley of the same name, which is known for its perfect chili-growing terrain. Every September, their harvest prompts special DIY roasting barrels at local markets, countless shipments all over the world, peel-and-roast parties, and festivals. I know many former New Mexico residents who hotly await their annual shipment no matter where they've relocated—and they will turn their nose up at lesser Anaheims. Hatch chilies come in a range of heats, so you can fine-tune your order from mild to spicy. You can also pay a little extra to purchase them pre-roasted, seeded, and chopped at Hatch-Chile.com, but once you've roasted your own Hatch chilies—when the mouth-wateringly herbaceous and smoky scent wafts throughout the house—you'll want to make it an annual tradition.

thai red ribs

serves 4 to 6

Traveling is a natural way to explore dishes and discover new flavors to love. It isn't always the exact recipe we bring home but the memory of it. If you tinker with a technique, like barbecuing ribs, and add new ingredients and seasoning combinations, you can hit upon a dish that contains the essence of your taste recollections. Our second-born son, Miles, toured Thailand at the age of eighteen. He'd already worked for two years in a professional kitchen and was a curious and resourceful cook. He picked up a couple of killer dishes during his trip, and made them his own. This is one of them. Check out the Shrimp Curry (page 108) for another. *Photo on page xii.*

4 Thai bird chilies or other small, hot chilies or 2 serrano chilies, seeded (if concerned about heat) and minced

1 whole head garlic, peeled and minced

6 scallions, diced

1 cup soy sauce

¾ cup rice wine or dry vermouth

¾ cup sugar

½ cup fish sauce

½ cup rice wine vinegar

1 teaspoon toasted sesame oil

4 racks pork spareribs, or 6 racks baby back ribs

1. Whisk together all the ingredients except the ribs in a large glass or ceramic dish. Add the ribs to the marinade, turn to coat, and marinate in the refrigerator for at least 1 hour and up to 3 hours. Turn the ribs in the marinade occasionally.

2. Prepare a grill for indirect heat: If using a charcoal grill, gather all the coals on one side of the grill. If using a gas grill, turn on one side of the heating element. The temperature should be around 250°F. (Or oven-roast them—see below.)

3. Place the ribs on the cooler section of the grill. Do not put them over the direct flame or heat source. Cover the grill and almost close the lid vents. Every 20 minutes, turn the ribs around to cook evenly and slather with the marinade. Spareribs should be perfectly cooked in 2½ to 3 hours; if using baby backs, count on 1½ to 2 hours. Let rest for 10 to 15 minutes, cut, and serve.

{

TO OVEN-ROAST:

Place the marinated ribs on a baking sheet and cook for 1½ to 2 hours at 350°F. Increase the heat to 425°F, brush with the marinade, and cook for 15 minutes more until caramelized.

}

ABOUT RIBS

It can be confusing to buy pork ribs. Here's what you need to know.

Baby backs are the smallest ribs, nestled up close to the backbone on the hog. They tend to be the most tender but least meaty. They're good for appetizers or dainty eaters, but if you need to feed a group of guys like I do, it's practically impossible to cook enough to satisfy everyone.

Spareribs are your best bet for feeding a throng of rib lovers. As you move further down the animal from the baby backs, the ribs get fatter and are set wider apart, with more meat between the bones and attached rib tips. The closer you get to the belly, the fattier the ribs are.

The St. Louis cut is similar to spareribs, except the rib tips have been cut off, creating a meaty yet slightly more refined presentation that is also a little easier to eat.

Regardless of type, plan on about 1 pound per person. Buy fresh meat if possible. I find that when ribs have been frozen, the meat tends to come off in whole strips, rather than bite by bite, and the frozen bone flavor is not my favorite (and ribs are all about the bone, after all!).

spicy-sweet ginger pork chops

serves 4 to 6

This speedy recipe is big on piquant flavor, as fresh ginger combines with the very spicy yet deeply floral taste of habanero chili. If you don't use too much of this chili, you can appreciate its flavor without being overwhelmed by its heat. Serve these chops with plain white rice or Coconut Rice (page 139), along with a salad or vegetable.

6 pork chops, about ½ to ¾ inch thick

Coarse salt

1 tablespoon safflower oil

3 onions, thinly sliced

4 garlic cloves, minced

One 3-inch piece of fresh ginger, peeled and sliced

½ teaspoon minced habanero or Scotch bonnet chili (from ¼ chili) or ½ teaspoon hot sauce from the same chili

½ cup flavorful liquid, such as wine, beer, or fruit juice

1 Heat a large heavy skillet over high heat. Generously season the chops with salt. Swirl half the oil in the skillet. When it shimmers, lay the pork chops in the pan and don't move them for at least a few minutes, to ensure that a golden sear forms. Turn and brown well on the second side for a total of 10 minutes. Transfer the chops to a warm plate.

2 Add the remaining oil and the onions, garlic, ginger, and chili, and cook until soft and lightly caramelized, 6 to 8 minutes. Return the chops to the pan, add the liquid, and cook until the chops are not quite firm to the touch, and an instant-read thermometer reads 138°F, 3 to 5 minutes more. Serve immediately.

BALANCING ACT

Pork chops are a quick, throw-together dinner. To ensure that you don't overcook them, start the rice before you begin the chops. Here's how: Bring the rice, water, and salt to a boil in the saucepan. Once you cover the rice to finish steaming, get started on browning the chops—they'll be done when the rice is ready. If you don't have the fresh ingredients for a salad or time to pull off a vegetable dish, put a handful of frozen peas and corn kernels on top of the rice during the last 5 minutes of cooking. Stir them into the rice before serving.

meal-in-one pork chops and greens

serves 4

Pork chops are the best riffing meat: as long as you brown and braise them without overcooking, lots of different preparations are possible using the browned pork as a base. You can then round out the pork's flavor with a sweet component such as apples or raisins. Braising greens with the chops adds an earthiness to the dish and makes it a complete meal.

4 pork chops (1 inch thick; about 3 pounds total)

Coarse salt and freshly ground black pepper

2 tablespoons extra-virgin olive oil

2 anchovy fillets (optional)

½ cup white wine or beer

1 cup chicken broth

1 bunch broccoli rabe (about 1 pound), trimmed and thinly sliced

¼ cup golden raisins

1 tablespoon unsalted butter

1 Preheat the oven to 375°F. Heat a 12-inch cast-iron skillet or oven-safe pan over high heat. Season the chops with salt and pepper on both sides. Swirl the oil in the skillet. When it shimmers, add the chops and sear until browned, about 3 minutes per side. Move the chops to the edges of the pan. If using, add the anchovies to the center of the pan, mash them up with a spatula or a spoon, and allow them to melt. Pour in the wine to deglaze the pan. Move the chops back to the center of the pan and add the broth, broccoli rabe, and raisins. Transfer the skillet to the oven. Cook until the chops register 138°F on an instant-read thermometer, 10 to 13 minutes (the carryover heat will bring them to 140°F).

2 Transfer the chops and broccoli rabe to a serving platter. (If the broccoli rabe isn't tender, let it cook on the stovetop for a few minutes.) Return the pan to the stovetop and boil the sauce until reduced by half. Swirl in the butter and pour the pan sauce over the chops.

ABOUT PRESERVED ANCHOVIES

If you love a mysterious flavor in any given dish but you can't quite put your finger on what it is, chances are a cured anchovy is involved. These earthy, salty little fishies liven up the deep flavor of almost any savory dish. Just don't tell anyone you're using anchovies (especially kids)—what they don't know won't hurt them, and a cured anchovy fillet will dissolve during cooking, leaving behind only a rich (non-fishy!) depth of tastiness.

Add 1 anchovy fillet or ½ teaspoon of anchovy paste:

when the onions and garlic are cooking for a **tomato sauce** ★ after the meat is browned for **chili** ★ with the mustard in a **vinaigrette dressing** ★ during the beginning stage of a **pan sauce** ★ mashed with a pinch of salt and diluted with a cup of water for a quick **fish stock**

wiener schnitzel

serves 6 to 8

Breaded. Browned. Well seasoned. No wonder these crispy meat cutlets are so beloved. Best of all, you can prepare them in advance: Layer the breaded, uncooked cutlets between pieces of parchment or wax paper, place in a resealable plastic bag, and store in the freezer for up to 2 months. Pull them out as needed and cook directly from frozen, adding 2 minutes more per side to the cooking time.

1 pork tenderloin (about 1½ pounds), sliced into 20 pieces

Coarse salt

3 large eggs

2 teaspoons Dijon mustard

¾ cup all-purpose flour

Freshly ground black pepper

3 slices white bread, processed into bread crumbs

2 tablespoons vegetable oil

2 tablespoons unsalted butter

1 lemon, cut into wedges, for serving

1 Lightly flatten each piece of pork with a meat mallet or the flat side of a small skillet. Season with salt. Beat the eggs with the mustard in a flat dish. Mix the flour with ½ teaspoon each salt and pepper in another flat dish. Place the bread crumbs in a third dish. Place the dishes side by side. Coat each piece of pork in flour, egg, and then bread crumbs.

2 Heat a large sauté pan over medium-high heat. Swirl in 1 tablespoon of the oil and 1 tablespoon of the butter. Add half of the cutlets and cook until golden and cooked through, 2 to 3 minutes per side. Transfer to a paper towel–lined plate. Wipe out the pan and repeat the process with the second batch. Serve the medallions on a warm platter with wedges of lemon for garnish.

WORTH KNOWING

HOW TO USE SALT

Salt makes food taste good. Period. It enhances natural flavors all on its own— and is not married to pepper for life! Here's a little primer on cookbook-speak when it comes to salt: When you're told to "season," think winter season, and add salt like a fine dusting of snow. Picture a "pinch" as a hefty snowflake. And boiling water for pasta or potatoes should taste salty like the sea.

double-decker pork tacos

makes 1 taco

At the famous La Taqueria in San Francisco's now trendy Mission District, the *dorados con todo*—or "doubles"—deserve their enthusiastic following: two tortillas layered with melted cheese are stuffed with various fillings. When you make them at home, you might want to swap in something else you have on hand—a few good options include Green Pork Chili (page 8) and the fillings from Pepper Steak Fajitas (page 34) or Spicy Shrimp Tacos (page 106). In one bite you get the lovely softness of steamed masa, melted cheese, *and* a golden crispy crunch. It's genius. I observed the on-site expert making them, one after another, until I gathered enough intel to create a home-style version.

2 teaspoons vegetable oil or lard

2 corn tortillas

1 slice mild, melting cheese, such as Monterey Jack, or Mexican melting cheese, such as queso asadero

¼ cup cooked chorizo, cubed

¼ white onion, chopped

1 tablespoon salsa, homemade (see below) or store-bought

1. Heat a large (preferably cast-iron) skillet over high heat. Swirl in 1 teaspoon of the oil and sauté the chorizo and onions until the onions are soft and golden. Transfer the chorizo and onions to a plate and wipe the skillet clean.

2. Add the remaining 1 teaspoon oil and place the tortillas in the pan. When the bottoms are toasted, about 1 minute, flip them both over.

3. Place the cheese on a tortilla. Take the other tortilla and place the toasted side against the cheese. Cook until the cheese has completely melted. Add the chorizo and salsa, fold over, and serve.

SALSA SIMPLIFIED

For a quick throw-together salsa, coarsely chop a small white onion and a small tomato. Mince one jalapeño pepper (seeded, if you're concerned about the heat). Mix all the ingredients together with a pinch of salt and ¼ cup water.

sunday gravy pocket pies

makes about 10 pocket pies

Pasta topped with a rich, meat-filled tomato sauce—typically called "gravy"—is a standard of Italian Sunday suppers. I like to use a simplified (and quicker) version of the same thick sauce to fill pocket pies, with the dough playing the role of the pasta. They are easy to make ahead of time and great to have on hand. Once assembled, you can freeze the raw pies for up to 2 months and then bake them straight from the freezer, adding 10 minutes to the baking time. Leftovers from Green Pork Chili (page 8), Cacciatore (page 59), or the Steak Pizzaiola from *Mad Hungry: Feeding Men & Boys* also make awesome fillings for pocket pies—just fill and bake as directed below.

THE FILLING

1 tablespoon olive oil

½ onion, chopped

3 garlic cloves, minced

1 pound ground pork

¼ cup sundried tomatoes, rehydrated (see page 20) or oil-packed in a jar, minced

¾ teaspoon coarse salt

One 14½-ounce can whole tomatoes and their juices, chopped

1 large basil sprig (optional)

½ cup grated Pecorino Romano or Parmesan cheese

8 ounces mozzarella, cut into small cubes (optional)

THE DOUGH

2 cups all-purpose flour

1 teaspoon coarse salt

1 cup (2 sticks) very cold unsalted butter, cut into pieces

½ cup cold water

1 large egg, for egg wash

1 Make the filling: Heat a medium saucepan over medium-high heat. Swirl in the oil. When it shimmers, add the onion and garlic, sautéing until the onion is translucent, about 4 minutes. Add the pork and cook, breaking it up into small pieces, until the moisture has evaporated and the meat is opaque and starting to brown, 7 to 8 minutes.

2 Stir in the sundried tomatoes and salt. Add the canned tomatoes and stir to mix, scraping the bottom of the pan to incorporate the browned bits left behind. Bring to a boil, then reduce the heat, partially cover, and simmer for 20 minutes. If the mixture gets too dry, add ¼ cup water to loosen it slightly. Remove the cover, add the basil sprig, if using, and cook for 10 minutes more. Remove the sauce from the heat, and stir in the grated cheese. Let cool. Stir in the mozzarella, if using. The filling can be covered and refrigerated for up to a few days at this point.

3 Meanwhile, make the dough: In a large bowl or in the bowl of a food processor, combine the flour and salt. Add the butter and cut it in (with your fingers, a fork, or a pastry cutter) or pulse until the mixture resembles a coarse meal. (To *cut in* means to mix cold fat such as butter with dry ingredients to form small pieces.) Pour in the water. Mix just until the dough holds together in a ball. Cut the dough in half, wrap in plastic wrap, and chill for 15 minutes. (If you are not using the dough right away, refrigerate it until you are ready to bake. Remove from the refrigerator at least 15 minutes before rolling it out.)

4 Preheat the oven to 375°F. Line a baking sheet with parchment paper or a silicone baking pad. To form the pies, work with half the dough at a time, rolling it out on a floured surface until it is about ⅛ inch thick. Using an overturned bowl (about 5 inches across), cut out 3 or 4 circles from each piece of dough. After cutting circles from both discs, gather together the dough scraps, and reroll once for the last circles.

5 Remove and discard the basil sprig from the filling (if you used one). Place ¼ cup of the filling on one side of a dough circle. Wet the edges of the dough with water and fold it over to form a half circle. Pinch the edges of the dough together and then crimp with a fork. Repeat with the remaining dough circles and filling. Put the pies on the prepared baking sheet. The pies can be frozen at this point (brush them with the egg wash described below before baking).

6 Chill the prepared pies on the baking sheet for a few minutes. When ready to bake, prepare your egg wash: beat the egg with 1 tablespoon water, and brush over each pie. Prick each pie twice with a fork. Bake until golden brown, 20 to 25 minutes. Let rest for 5 minutes before serving. These pies can be cooled and frozen. Reheat in the oven or microwave.

WORTH KNOWING

HOW TO REHYDRATE SUNDRIED TOMATOES

To soften, place the sundried tomatoes in a heat-proof container. Pour boiling water over the tomatoes and let sit for 5 minutes. Drain. Rehydrated tomatoes can be stored in the refrigerator, covered with olive oil, for up to 2 months.

SMELL IS THE MOST TRANSPORTING SENSE

In an instant, one whiff can trigger the memory of how it *felt* in your childhood kitchen. Proust had his madeleines; I have Faico's Pork Store on Bleecker Street in New York's Greenwich Village. I take one step in and I am overcome with a long-ago feeling, sparked by the heady aroma of provolone, Pecorino Romano, Parmesan, pork, garlic, and tomato sauce.

In a single inhale, I instantly time-travel back to my Italian grandmother's kitchen: she and her sisters, my great-aunts, are once again bustling around in their floral house dresses, amid chatter, laughter, and hand gestures, while meatballs bubble away in their pots of "Sunday sauce."

Of course, that Sunday sauce was one of the first things I learned to cook, and thank goodness I did—it's like a piece of amber encasing the happiness of my childhood. Making that sauce is also the closest I'll ever come to transporting my sons back to my own past, or introducing them to their great-grandmother, whom I loved so much and who is now forty years gone.

If there is a dish you loved growing up, take time to find out how to make it. Someday you'll want to know how to cook that chicken soup. And get specific about ingredients: Shake down your mom for the exact ratios of her tuna salad, because no one else's sandwich tastes so good. For the love of God, get the name of her mayonnaise brand! And don't turn up your nose— or reach for an alternative—when she names the off-brand label.

If no one in your family cooked, it's time to make your own food memories. Cook what you love, make it again and again—and notice how it makes those around you happy.

maple pigs in a blanket

makes 18 pieces

Almost everyone loves a good pig in a blanket. These piglets make a pop-in-your-mouth breakfast snack just as easily as they do a cocktail nibble. Store-bought puff pastry pulled from the freezer is your flaky friend, as it will thaw in 30 minutes and be ready to roll, stuff, wrap, or layer.

1 sheet puff pastry, thawed according to package instructions

2 tablespoons maple syrup, plus more for serving

18 cooked small breakfast sausage links (about 1 pound)

1 large egg

1 Preheat the oven to 425°F with the rack in the center position. Line a baking sheet with parchment paper, foil, or a silicone baking pad.

2 Roll out the puff pastry to a 12-inch square. Brush the maple syrup over the entire surface of the pastry. Cut the dough into thirds and then into thirds again to form 9 squares. Cut each square in half diagonally to make 18 triangles.

3 Place a breakfast sausage link on the lower third of each triangle and roll up, making sure to place each bundle seam side down on the lined baking sheet. Whisk together the egg and 1 teaspoon water in a small bowl. Brush each bundle with egg wash and bake until golden brown, 16 to 18 minutes. Serve immediately with maple syrup on the side.

ABOUT PUFF PASTRY

When a recipe calls for puff pastry, there is absolutely no need to panic or faint away with visions of the prolonged task of rolling and folding the dough from scratch. Even the best professional bakers I know recommend, without a single qualm, the frozen kind you find at the grocery store. Pepperidge Farm puff pastry, made with vegetable shortening, is the most widely available and makes a fine choice. Even better are the butter-based Dufour and Trader Joe's brands. If you can play with Play-Doh, you can work with puff pastry. Be sure to handle it when it's still slightly cool (if your kitchen is hot or the dough warms up, pop it in the fridge for about 10 minutes). When you're ready to roll out the dough, dust your counter and rolling pin (or a clean wine bottle if you don't have a pin) with a light coating of flour. Cut the rolled pastry into squares and fill them with jam or fruit or spinach and feta for turnovers—or cut into any shape your heart desires.

hamjam cheddar puffs

makes 18 pieces

When I'm putting together a multigenerational breakfast or brunch, I know the kids will eat a lot of these. A lot! Of course, these savory-sweet treats are an any-meal, anytime choice. The full flavors of the mustard and sharp Cheddar cheese set off the sweet berry jam in a deliciously savory way.

1 sheet puff pastry, thawed according to package instructions

2 tablespoons Dijon mustard

3 ounces sharp Cheddar cheese, shredded

¼ teaspoon freshly ground black pepper

4 to 5 ounces ham, cut into 18 matchsticks (about ¼ inch wide by 3 inches long)

⅓ cup favorite jam (I like apricot)

1 large egg

1 Preheat the oven to 425°F with the rack in the center position. Line a baking sheet with parchment paper, foil, or a silicone baking pad.

2 Roll out the puff pastry to a 12-inch square. Brush the mustard over the entire surface of the pastry and sprinkle with the cheese and pepper. Cut the dough into thirds and then into thirds again to make 9 squares. Cut each square in half diagonally to make 18 triangles.

3 Place a piece of ham on the lower third of each triangle, add a small spoonful of jam, and roll up. Place each bundle seam side down on the lined baking sheet. Whisk together the egg and 1 teaspoon water in a small bowl. Brush each bundle with egg wash and bake until golden brown, 16 to 18 minutes. Serve immediately.

prosciutto grilled cheese

makes 1 sandwich

Use this technique for any sandwich that calls for a golden, crispy outside and melty, gooey inside. If you don't have two cast-iron skillets (or a panini press), weight the sandwich with another pan or plate (if the pan or plate is not heavy, weight it with a of couple of cans of soup or beans). When the bottom is golden, flip the sandwich and repeat on the other side, weighted as before. Choose a firm-textured bread.

2 slices sturdy Italian bread

2 tablespoons extra-virgin olive oil

1 tablespoon balsamic vinegar

Two ¼-inch-thick slices mozzarella

Two ¼-inch-thick slices ripe tomato

1 slice prosciutto

2 tablespoons finely shredded fresh basil

2 tablespoons unsalted butter, at room temperature

1 Heat two cast-iron pans over high heat. Lay the bread slices side by side on a work surface and drizzle with the oil and vinegar. Top one piece of bread with a slice of mozzarella, the tomato slices, prosciutto, basil, and the remaining slice of mozzarella. Close the sandwich and spread half the butter on the top slice.

2 Place the sandwich, buttered side down, in one of the pans and quickly spread the remaining butter over the top of the sandwich. Using a pot holder or kitchen towel, place the other hot pan on top of the sandwich and press gently. Reduce the heat to low and cook, continuing to press, until the sandwich is golden brown and the cheese has melted, about 4 minutes. Serve immediately.

{

ALSO GREAT WITH:

baked ham ★ mortadella ★ sopressata ★ Genoa salami ★ pepperoni ★ cooked pancetta or bacon

}

NOTES TO A NOVICE: BEFORE YOU COOK

I'm watching my youngest son cook from my first Mad Hungry book—the book with the recipes that raised and fed him.

For a guy who knows how to cook a little, he doesn't seem to notice that the weight of the meat (that he's scrounged from our fridge) is twice that called for in the recipe. Thankfully, he realizes midway through that he needs to double the marinade ingredients to accommodate the amount of meat. I butt in to state what I thought was obvious: if you plan to make more than a recipe calls for, it is a good idea to know this before you begin cooking. Reading the recipe beforehand is always essential.

My son confesses that his most challenging cooking problem by far is planning his time so that multiple elements finish together. It's a dance of timing to be plotted before you start. As experience is gained, the whole coordination becomes second nature. Here are a few tips:

Do all the prep work before you start cooking, no matter how simple the recipes may seem. Pull the ingredients out, make a plan, and measure, chop, squeeze—whatever needs to be done—all before even approaching the stove. If both a steak's marinade and the potatoes call for garlic, chop it all at once. If there's parsley in the recipe, chop it after the garlic, as it neutralizes the odor left behind on the chopping board (same goes for your breath, by the way).

Make sure you have the pan, tool, ingredient, or heat source you need to complete the chosen task *before* you begin the actual cooking.

If cooking several dishes, start the recipe that takes the longest first. If you're cooking meat, factor in an extra 30 minutes so it has time out of the refrigerator to temper. (No, it's not absolutely essential, but the meat will cook a little more evenly.) Making spinach? It may be really gritty and require two to four water baths to clean. This is hands-on and time-consuming, so do it before you start anything else. Making rice? You have 20 minutes (or longer) to cook everything else because, if tightly lidded, the rice will stay hot for 10 to 15 minutes after it's finished. Searing a steak to rare? You'll want it to rest for 5 to 8 minutes after cooking and before eating, so it will likely be the very last thing you cook.

Consider heating your plates when serving hot food. Either heat ceramic plates in a 200°F oven for 10 minutes, run them under hot water (dry them before using), heat for a minute in the microwave, or place them on top of a warm stove.

broiled black pepper sirloin steak

serves 2 to 4

Eat with brothers, sons, or other males on the regular, and you'll eat a lot of steak. I am forever figuring out new ways to make meat. My aim: something that accentuates steak's beefiness but isn't too complicated. I love broiling, but in order for it to work well, you need to remove the steak from the refrigerator 30 minutes in advance so it is close to room temperature; otherwise, the meat steams before broiling and becomes gray and not so tasty.

Extra-virgin olive oil, for drizzling

1½ pounds boneless sirloin steak (¾ to 1 inch thick)

Coarse salt and freshly ground black pepper

1 onion, halved and sliced

1 tablespoon unsalted butter

⅓ cup red wine vinegar

1 Preheat the broiler. Place a large oven-proof skillet (preferably cast-iron) as close to the broiler as possible and let it heat for 2 minutes. Drizzle the steaks with oil and rub it over the meat. Season both sides generously with salt and pepper. Add the steak to the heated skillet and broil for 6 to 8 minutes (6 minutes for medium-rare). Transfer the steak to a plate to rest.

2 Heat the empty skillet on the stovetop over medium heat. Add the onions and butter. Stir and cook until browned, about 6 minutes. Pour in the vinegar and scrape up the browned bits on the bottom of the skillet. Simmer the vinegar until reduced, about 1 minute. Pour any steak juices from the resting steak into the skillet and remove from the heat. Transfer the steak to a cutting board and cut into ¼-inch-thick slices. Lay the steak slices on a platter, pour the sauce over top, and serve.

LIVESAVER LESSON

PREHEAT THE PAN

When you're broiling or oven-frying—anytime you want a good sear or a caramelized crust on meat or vegetables without frying or sautéing—place your pan or baking sheet into the hot oven to preheat it before placing the food on it. When the pan is good and hot, you'll hear a satisfying sizzle when the food hits it, which hastens the formation of a seared golden seal on the food.

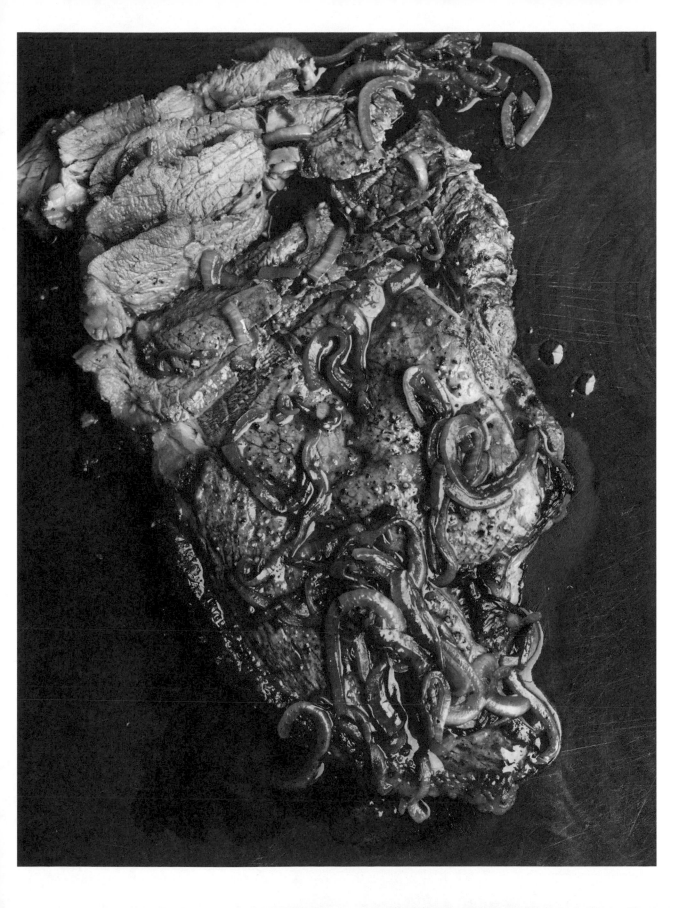

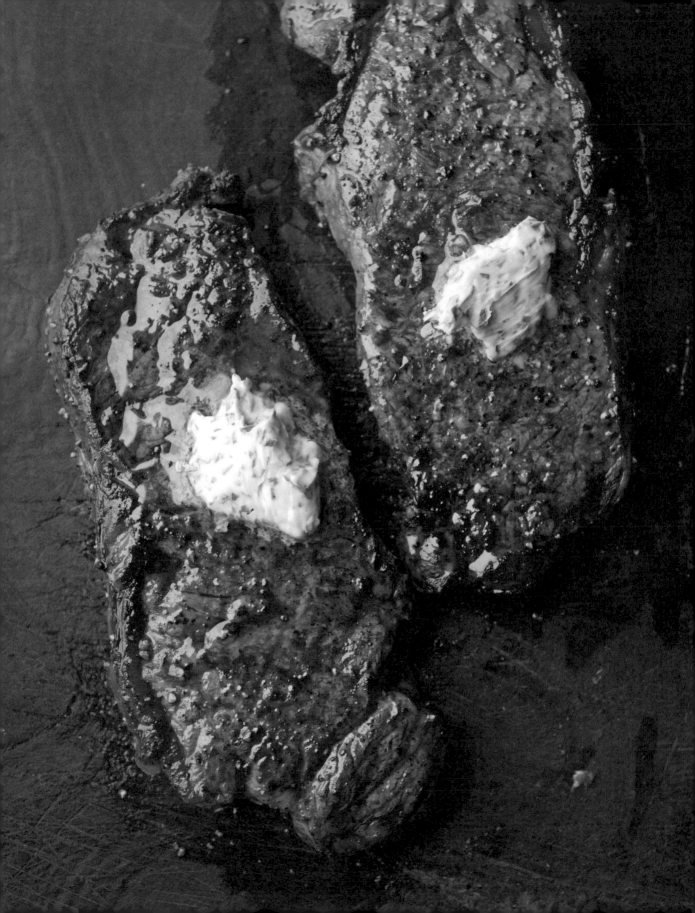

grilled strip steak with herb butter

serves 2

Make some of this easy compound butter to keep in the fridge—it dresses up plain seared steak, pork chops, chicken, or fish. Drop a pat of it onto the piping-hot meat and it will melt into an instant sauce that is both bright and satisfyingly rich. Feel free to play around—any chopped fresh herb can be added to the butter, and it's a good way to use up those bunches of mint or parsley that have been languishing in the crisper. If you don't have a grill or grill pan, just panfry your steak following the instructions on page 32.

THE HERB BUTTER

3 tablespoons unsalted butter, softened

3 tablespoons chopped fresh parsley leaves

1 small garlic clove, minced

2 strip steaks (¾ inch thick; about 1 pound total)

Coarse salt and freshly ground black pepper

1 Mash together the butter, parsley, and garlic in a small bowl. Chill until just firm. Prepare the grill, or preheat a grill pan over high heat. Generously season the steaks on both sides with salt and pepper. Cook on a high-heat grill or grill pan for 3 minutes without moving the meat. Turn and cook for 3 minutes more for medium-rare, about 135°F on a meat thermometer.

2 Remove the steaks from the grill and let rest for a few minutes. Top each steak with a generous pat of herb butter. Serve hot.

FLAVORED BUTTERS

Start with 3 tablespoons of softened, unsalted butter and a pinch of salt.

Make it spicy: add ⅛ teaspoon cayenne pepper or minced hot red chili.

Make it tangy: add ¼ teaspoon finely grated lemon, lime, or orange zest.

Make it earthy: add 1 tablespoon sautéed chopped mushrooms and shallots.

Make it savory: add ½ teaspoon miso paste.

Make it sweet: add 1 teaspoon honey mustard.

BESPOKE SAUCE

asian pantry marinated steak

serves 4

So many pantries contain those odd ingredients that are only used three or four times a year—
at best!—for a specific recipe. (I've heard of jugs of oyster sauce outlasting some marriages!)
This recipe aims to keep some of those lesser-used Asian condiments in more frequent rotation
by teaming them up so they complement one another in a perfectly balanced marinade. See
"Ingredient Substitutions" on page 6 for more marinade options. This marinade is also good
with pork chops.

3 tablespoons hoisin sauce

3 tablespoons mirin

1½ tablespoons fish sauce

2 teaspoons rice wine vinegar

1 teaspoon toasted sesame oil

4 small minute steaks, or one 2-pound
London broil

1 teaspoon vegetable oil

1 lime, cut into wedges, for serving

Sriracha hot sauce, for serving

1 Whisk together the hoisin, mirin, fish
sauce, and sesame oil in a shallow dish or
baking pan. Pat dry the steaks and add to
the marinade, turning a couple of times.
Marinate the steaks for 15 to 20 minutes at
room temperature.

2 Heat a large skillet over high heat. Swirl in
the vegetable oil. When it shimmers, add
the steak (reserving the marinade). If using
minute steaks, cook for 3 minutes without
moving, then turn and cook for about
3 minutes more for medium-rare. If using
a London broil, increase cooking times
to 4 and 5 minutes, respectively. Add the
reserved marinade to the skillet for the last
2 minutes of cooking.

3 If using a London broil, transfer the meat
to a cutting board, lightly tent with foil,
and let rest for 5 minutes before slicing and
serving. You can serve the minute steaks
directly. Serve the steaks with the lime
wedges and hot sauce.

ONE BIG STEAK TO SERVE THEM ALL

While it is nice to have your very own steak, a good cut is expensive—definitely not a very economical way to feed a group.

If you are using a marinade, which will flavor and tenderize the meat, buy one affordable large steak, and slice it to serve in portions. Look for:

Top or bottom round sirloin: top round is slightly more tender than the bottom, but both have good flavor and are great candidates for marinating.

Tri-tip steak: from the sirloin section, the tri-tip contains less marbling than other cuts, so take care not to overcook it.

Flank steak: from the "flank" of the steer, this lean cut should be cooked quickly in order to be juicy, no more than medium-rare. Slice it thinly against the grain to serve.

Flat iron or blade steak: one of the most underrated and hardest to find of the affordable cuts, this is a very tender choice compared to others from the sirloin section.

London broil: many steaks, including some of the thin and less tender cuts mentioned above, are mislabeled as London broil. It originally was a term that referred to a way of preparing flank steak. Cook London broil to any desired doneness, but slice it thinly against the grain before serving.

Cube steak: also known as minute steak, this is a tough cut of beef that has been tenderized by pounding or running it through a machine to break down the fibers. We often ate this inexpensive cut with a teriyaki marinade when I was growing up, and I loved it.

pepper steak fajitas

serves 4 to 6

You don't have to go to a restaurant for fajitas—this beloved (if ubiquitous) Tex-Mex dish is easy to make at home with sliced beef, a few vegetables, and a stack of tortillas. Top round steak is typical for fajitas, but flank, skirt, or hanger steak, thinly sliced across the grain, work equally well. This beef mixture is also a delicious filling alternative for Double-Decker Pork Tacos (page 16).

4 garlic cloves, minced

Juice of 2 limes

1½ pounds top round steaks, pounded and scored with a knife tip in a crosshatch pattern, or skirt steak

Coarse salt and freshly ground black pepper

1 tablespoon vegetable oil

1 red or green bell pepper, cored, seeded, and sliced

1 onion, sliced

12 flour or corn tortillas, warmed

1 Combine the garlic and lime juice in a small bowl and set aside. Heat a large heavy skillet (preferably cast-iron) over high heat. Generously season the meat on both sides with salt and black pepper.

2 Swirl half the oil in the hot skillet. When it shimmers, add the meat and sear for 2 minutes on each side for medium-rare. Transfer the steaks to a plate (leaving the skillet on the heat), and pour the garlic-lime mixture over them.

3 Reduce the heat to medium-high and swirl the remaining oil in the skillet. Add the bell peppers and onions and sauté until soft and golden brown around the edges, 8 to 10 minutes.

4 Slice the steak and return it to the skillet along with any accumulated juices. Serve the fajitas in the skillet with the tortillas on the side.

GROUND BEEFINESS

If filet mignon is the little black dress of beef cuts, then ground beef is the blue jeans. We all use it, it tends to go unnoticed, but it's essential to our wardrobe. Once the premium steak and roasts have been cut off, ground beef is made from the leftover scraps and tougher cuts. Supermarkets generally package ground beef made from chuck, round, or sirloin, all with varying degrees of fat (usually between 20 percent for chuck and 10 percent for sirloin).

These days, it's all the rage to combine different cuts into a custom burger blend that strikes a perfect balance of flavor, texture, and fat. Sirloin, skirt, and hanger steaks bring that predictable beefy-nutty flavor; chuck, short rib, and brisket also deliver the fat needed to keep the meat moist and tender. A butcher can make the blend for you, but if you want to get all nerdy about it, invest in the grinder attachment for the Kitchen-Aid mixer, or get yourself a home-style meat grinder. If you are good with standard grocery store ground meat, pick the best quality you can afford—with no preservatives, phosphates, or binders (remember when that nasty "pink slime" made the news?). As for fat content, bear in mind that grass-fed beef has very little fat, so it dries out easily if overcooked.

Meatballs and Meat Loaf

In most recipes for meatballs and meat loaf, ground meat is mixed with bread crumbs to stretch and lighten the meat. I have found that dry bread crumbs make dry meatballs—they don't add moisture while sucking up what little there is in the meat. Solve this problem by soaking a few slices of stale bread in milk, squeezing them out, then mincing them and using these soggy bits in lieu of crumbs. An equal amount of mashed potatoes will also work.

I love to add onions to meatballs and meat loaf and prefer to grate rather than chop them. Grated onions melt into a good, oniony juice, which adds a shot of moisture. As you're shaping the meatballs or loaf, don't overwork the mixture or you'll end up with tough texture. Mix it just enough to marry the elements and distribute the seasoning. When forming multiple meatballs, keep a bowl of cold water nearby and periodically dunk your hands in it to keep the mixture from sticking to your hands as you roll.

continued

Basic Meatball Roadmap

For about fifteen 1½-inch meatballs, you need: 1 pound ground meat, 1 large egg, 1 tablespoon grated onion, 1 minced garlic clove, 1 slice milk-soaked bread, squeezed and minced, ½ cup grated Parmesan or Pecorino Romano cheese, and ½ teaspoon salt. Combine the mixture. Roll into 1½-inch balls. Brown or drop into bubbling-hot Simple Tomato Sauce (page 120) until cooked through.

Basic Meat Loaf Roadmap

For 1 meat loaf, you need: 2 pounds ground meat, 2 slices milk-soaked bread, squeezed and minced, ¼ cup grated onion, 1 beaten egg, 1 small grated carrot, 2 teaspoons salt, and ½ teaspoon freshly ground black pepper. Pack the mixture into an 8½-by-4½-inch loaf pan. Brush ketchup or chili sauce on top. Bake at 325°F for 40 to 45 minutes.

Hamburgers

Good burgers are an essential main course in many households, and a great-tasting burger needs fat. For a basic Wednesday night burger, I prefer ground chuck (usually about 20 percent fat), which has a good balance of juicy fat and meaty texture. (If I have a leaner ground meat on hand, I usually mince a few slices of raw bacon to mix into the beef.)

The best way to ensure that the fat blends with the meat's juices and stays inside the patty is to cook the patty (well-seasoned with lots of salt and pepper) on super high heat. This sears the outside and seals in those precious juices. Don't press down on the hamburgers with a spatula during cooking—that makes the juices run out. If you like a thin patty, roll it out with a rolling pin or a clean bottle before cooking. Cook the patties for about 3 minutes without moving them; flip the burgers and cook until done, about 4 minutes more. Remove the patties from the pan and let sit for a minute before building the burger. Of course, thinner patties will need less cooking time.

BTW: the bun is key. You need bread that will absorb (not disintegrate from) the juices as you bite in. Hands down, Martin's potato rolls are my favorite. I like them butter-toasted on the inside, soft and steamy on the outside.

Chili and Meat Sauce for Pasta

A good pot of chili and a delicious meat sauce for pasta start with a lean ground sirloin and will likely contain an array of sautéed aromatic ingredients (onion, garlic, carrot, celery), and require a long simmering time. In both cases, add the spices to the meat while it's browning to infuse it with flavor and transform the raw taste. After browning, what little fat the sirloin has is released. Drain off some of it (for health) and leave a bit (for flavor).

Basic Meat Sauce Roadmap

Mince ½ cup each of celery and onion, a small carrot, and a small amount of garlic. Slowly and constantly stir the vegetables in a little olive oil in a skillet or sauté pan over medium-high heat until soft and just starting to caramelize. Add the ground meat (about 1 pound of beef, pork, veal, or any combo), and cook until browned. First, press down on the meat clumps with a spatula to break them up and help brown them. As you stir, the meat will release its juices. Add some tomato paste, stir for a couple of minutes, and then slosh in some wine (red or white). Simmer until the wine has mostly evaporated. If you have some great stock on hand, add a cup or more to moisten the mixture. Let the sauce simmer a bit. Add a can of crushed tomatoes, pulse in a blender, and let the sauce bubble away until slightly thickened, 30 to 45 minutes. Season to taste with salt and pepper.

Basic Chili Roadmap

Sauté a couple of chopped onions and minced garlic cloves in oil, then add 2 pounds of ground beef and cook until browned. Stir in 1 teaspoon each of ground cumin, salt, and dried oregano, a pinch of crushed red pepper flakes, and a couple of tablespoons of chili powder. Cook for a few minutes. Add a large can of tomatoes and a bottle of beer. Simmer for about 1 hour, adding a small can of drained red beans for the last 15 minutes.

shepherd's pie

serves 6

In his autobiography, Rolling Stones guitarist Keith Richards tells of cooking two things at home: bangers and mash (sausage and mashed potatoes), and shepherd's pie. Here, I have co-opted his idea of doubling up on the onions by adding a bonus layer of chopped, raw onions between the cooked onion–meat mixture and the potatoes. Save on dishes by sautéing the meat mixture in the same oven-safe, deep skillet you will bake the pie in. Alternatively, sauté the meat in a skillet and assemble the pie in a separate casserole dish.

5 medium potatoes, such as Idaho or russet, peeled and roughly chopped into 2-inch pieces

Coarse salt

8 tablespoons (1 stick) unsalted butter

2 carrots, chopped

1 celery stalk, chopped

1 large onion, finely chopped

2 pounds ground lamb or beef, or a combo

Freshly ground black pepper

¼ cup Worcestershire sauce

¾ cup chicken or beef broth

2 teaspoons cornstarch

½ cup milk, plus more if needed

1 cup frozen peas, thawed and drained

1 Place the potatoes in a large pot and add enough cold water to cover by 2 inches. Add a generous amount of coarse salt. Bring to a boil and cook until tender enough to mash, 15 to 20 minutes.

2 Preheat the oven to 400°F.

3 Meanwhile, melt 2 tablespoons of the butter in a 10-inch oven-safe skillet (preferably cast-iron) over medium-high heat. Add the carrots, celery, and half the onion and sauté until softened, about 4 minutes.

Add the meat and 2 teaspoons salt and cook over high heat, pressing and stirring to break up the meat, until the moisture has evaporated and the meat is browning in fat, about 15 minutes. (The skillet will seem overly full but the mixture will cook down.) When the meat is browned, stir in the Worcestershire sauce and cook for 1 minute.

4 Whisk together the broth and cornstarch in a small bowl and add to the meat mixture. Simmer for an additional minute to thicken.

5 Drain the potatoes, setting aside ½ cup of the cooking water. Return the potatoes to the pot. Add the reserved cooking water, milk, and 4 tablespoons of the butter and season with pepper. Mash until smooth. Add more milk if needed to achieve a smooth, spreadable texture.

6 Spread the meat mixture around in the bottom of the pan it was cooked in or transfer to a 2-quart casserole dish. Evenly distribute the peas and remaining onion over the meat. Dollop and spread the mashed potatoes over the vegetables. Dot the top of the potatoes with the remaining 2 tablespoons butter.

7 Bake until heated through, the potatoes are golden on top, and the filling is bubbling, about 30 minutes.

beef-stuffed peppers and squash

serves 8

Stuffing a ground meat mixture into a vegetable such as bell peppers or squash yields a complete meal, and it's no wonder that practically every culture has a version, tailoring the seasonings and sauce to their own particular traditions. Rice is such a useful way to stretch the ground meat without sacrificing flavor, especially if the dish is already well seasoned. Sometimes I make a double batch of the filling and freeze half, which streamlines the prep the next time I make this dish—defrost, stuff, bake, dinner!

2 cups Simple Tomato Sauce (page 120), plus more for serving

1 tablespoon extra-virgin olive oil, plus more for drizzling

2 large shallots, or 1 onion, diced

4 garlic cloves, minced

2 pounds ground meat (any combo of beef, pork, and/or veal)

2 cups cooked white rice (see page 136)

⅓ cup almonds, walnuts, or pine nuts, toasted (optional)

⅓ cup currants or raisins (optional)

2 teaspoons coarse salt

Freshly ground black pepper

5 bell peppers (any combo of yellow, red, orange, or green), tops sliced off and seeds removed

3 delicata or acorn squash, halved lengthwise and seeds removed (or just use more peppers)

1. Preheat the oven to 375°F. Make the tomato sauce. Heat a small skillet over medium-high heat and swirl in the oil. Add the shallots and garlic. Sauté for about 2 minutes to soften. Transfer to a large bowl.

2. Add the meat, rice, pine nuts, currants (if using), and salt to the bowl, and season with black pepper. Mix well. Season the inside of the bell peppers and squash with salt and black pepper. Stuff the meat mixture into the squash and bell peppers. Add about 1 tablespoon tomato sauce to the top of each vegetable. Pour ¾ cup of the tomato sauce over the bottom of one large or two small pans, and arrange the bell peppers and squash snugly in the pan(s). Drizzle with oil and cover with foil.

3. Bake until the squash is tender, the peppers are soft, and the meat is cooked through, 45 minutes to 1 hour (depending on the size and thickness of the vegetables). Raise the heat to 425°F, remove the foil, and baste the vegetables with the pan sauce. Cook until the vegetables start to caramelize on top, about 15 minutes more. Serve with extra sauce spooned around the cooked vegetables.

WAYS WITH THIS FILLING

Here are some more ideas for stuffed veggies:

Cabbage or kale leaves: blanch the leaves in salted boiling water, pat dry, and while they are still warm and supple, roll them up with the beef filling. Place the rolls side by side in a shallow casserole dish, spoon some Simple Tomato Sauce (page 120) over them, and bake in a 375°F oven until bubbling hot, about 40 minutes.

Zucchini or summer squash: slice the zucchini lengthwise, then scoop out and sauté the chopped pulp. Add it to the meat mixture while browning, season to taste, and spoon the filling into the scooped squashes. Bake in a 375°F oven until bubbling hot, about 40 minutes. If you want, spoon some tomato sauce over the filling before baking.

Tomatoes: these love a good filling like this meat one, especially when topped with crunchy, cheesy bread crumbs. Bake at 375°F for 40 to 45 minutes.

Onions: cut out the inside layers of the onions, leaving the outsides intact. Chop the inside layers and sauté in olive oil. When the onions soften, stir them into the meat filling. Brush the outside of the onions with olive oil and sprinkle with salt. Carefully spoon the stuffing in the onions and bake at 375°F until bubbling hot, about 45 minutes. As they bake, the onions will become caramelized golden vessels.

CHICKEN CONFIDENTIAL

OPPOSITE: Flat Roast Citrus Chicken (page 52)

POULTRY PREROGATIVE

What I love about chicken is the flexibility that a whole bird offers. I can roast it (page 51), flat roast it (page 52), or braise small pieces, as in Cacciatore (page 59). (Nothing beats a chicken braise for building a quick flavor base.) Well-seasoned, skin-on pieces, browned in butter or oil, lend depth of flavor and leave that golden fond behind in the pan. (Fond is the word for those tasty little bits left in a pan after meat, chicken, or fish is cooked.) The next step can take you in a million different directions depending on the liquid, vegetables, and seasonings you add.

A single chicken has so many elements that go into a tasty dish: lean white meat; richer, fattier dark meat; crunchiness from the skin; thickener from the cartilage; and finally, broth from the bones. I try to keep at least one chicken at all times in the fridge (it'll last a couple of days) or freezer (wrapping it well with foil or freezer paper over the store packaging buys you 9 to 12 months).

With a good solid sharp knife, the bird can be cut into one of many configurations; any butcher will happily oblige if you're not up to it. My rule of thumb: the more mouths to feed, the smaller the pieces (bones and all). Just make the final dish saucier and up the carb companion of rice, pasta, or polenta, and there will be plenty of flavor payoff for everyone. Add a few vegetable dishes to the meal, and reverse the standard ratio of protein on the plate.

If buying a whole bird is not your thing, there are a few "parts" that I particularly love. You can't beat chicken thighs for flavor. Yes, it's dark meat (breast lovers, stay with me here), but if you're braising, slow-roasting, or slow-cooking, thighs stand up to the heat, deliver the flavor, and result in an excellent moist texture. Boneless thighs are great for sandwiches (like Jerk Chicken and Mango Chutney Sandwiches, page 46) and casseroles (like Coq au Vin Casserole, page 68).

As for my own favorite part of the bird, I'm a wing girl. If we are feasting on a whole roast chicken for dinner, I am more than content to eat both of the wings. If there are wings at a party or on a bar menu, my husband knows where to find me! For at-home snacking with my brood, or any large gathering, I look for deals at the grocery store on large packages of wings (the exception to my "buy the whole bird" rule). Since they're so small—and nearly equal amounts skin, meat, and bone—the chicken flavor shines through in every bite.

Do not eat any old chicken, no matter how tired, broke, or pathetic you may feel. Invest in the best bird available: a free-range, antibiotic-free, massaged-daily, and hand-fed-with-an-eyedropper chicken. Okay, I'm sort of kidding. Just try to get the best chicken you can afford.

LIFESAVER LESSON

CHICKEN PARTS

For a dish like Arroz con Pollo (page 62) or Cacciatore (page 59), I like cutting a chicken into 16 pieces, because it means more pieces of meat and bone to distribute among a dish, which stretches the protein. It also exposes more surface area to the browning process, which enhances the yumminess of each piece of chicken and the flavor of the dish overall.

To get 16 pieces, take the eight natural chicken parts (2 legs, 2 thighs, 2 wings, and 2 breasts) and cut each one in half. You can easily do this at home with a sharp cleaver, or ask the butcher to do it for you. Most butchers or staffers at supermarket meat counters are happy to help. I always ask to have the wing tips and back reserved; I add them to a bag in the freezer, from which I'll draw later to make stock.

jerk chicken and mango chutney sandwiches

makes 12 sandwiches

Jamaica is my home away from home and has been for my whole life. After every visit, I try to re-create the new and favorite dishes I experienced—that way, the feeling of Jamaica stays with me throughout the year. This grab-and-go sandwich is my best taste-representation of the island: homemade jerk sauce flavors a chicken cutlet while tangy-sweet mango chutney offsets the spicy meat. I also like to spread a little coconut oil on each roll—it's not necessary but it's so, so good and adds to the tropical flavor of the sandwich. Serve these at a party with ice-cold beer. *Photo on page vi.*

5 bunches scallions, trimmed and roughly chopped

3 large garlic cloves, peeled

3 Scotch bonnet chili peppers (seeded, if concerned about the heat)

2 sprigs fresh thyme, leaves removed, or 2 teaspoons dried

¼ cup ground allspice

2 tablespoons freshly ground black pepper

1½ tablespoons coarse salt

½ cup water

4 pounds skinless, boneless chicken thighs, trimmed (and halved if pieces are too large to fit on bun)

12 soft hamburger rolls, such as Martin's potato rolls

¼ cup coconut oil (optional)

¾ cup mango chutney, homemade (recipe follows) or store-bought

1 Working in two batches, in the bowl of a food processor, combine the scallions, garlic, Scotch bonnet peppers, thyme leaves, allspice, pepper, and salt; pulse a few times for a rough texture. With the processor running, add ¼ cup of the water per batch through the feed tube to make a coarse sauce. Set aside ½ cup for serving. (Alternatively, the scallions, garlic, and peppers can be minced with a knife and combined with the remaining ingredients.)

2 Place the chicken in a large bowl, baking dish, or resealable plastic bag. Pour the sauce over the chicken, turning to coat. Pierce the chicken with a fork. Cover and refrigerate, turning occasionally, for at least 2 hours and up to 24 hours.

3 Prepare a grill, or place a grill pan over high heat. Place the chicken on a relatively cool part of the grill. If using a grill pan, reduce the heat to medium. Cook for 15 minutes, brushing the chicken with the marinade a

{

SWAP THE CHICKEN FOR:

boneless pork chops ★ firm-fleshed boneless white fish fillets like mahi-mahi or snapper (marinated for half the time) ★ ⅓-inch-thick slabs of eggplant

}

couple of times. Flip the chicken over and repeat the process until slightly charred and an instant-read thermometer reads 160°F, 15 minutes more. (Alternatively, preheat the oven to 425°F and bake for 40 minutes, turning once halfway through.) Remove from the heat and let rest for 10 minutes.

4 Spread some coconut oil on the inside of each roll. Put a piece of chicken on the bottom part of each roll and spread a tablespoon of chutney and the reserved sauce, as desired, on each before closing the roll and serving.

mango chutney

makes 3 cups

4 mangoes, peeled, pitted, and chopped (about 4 cups)

3 tablespoons grated fresh ginger

1 medium onion, chopped (about 2 cups)

1 garlic clove, minced

½ red bell pepper, chopped

⅓ cup sugar

2 teaspoons salt

½ cup white vinegar

⅓ cup water

½ cup raisins (optional)

Mix all the ingredients in a medium nonreactive pot. Bring to a boil over high heat, then reduce the heat to low and simmer, stirring occasionally, for 1 hour and 15 minutes. Remove the chutney from the heat and let cool. Store in the refrigerator for up to 2 months.

chicken and black bean nachos

serves 6 to 8

Nachos can stand an ingredient riff, but to make sure that the cheese is melted throughout and that each bite has the requisite combination of tastes and textures, follow this plan.

2 tablespoons safflower oil

1 small white onion, chopped

One 15-ounce can black beans, drained and rinsed

½ teaspoon ground cumin

¼ teaspoon dried oregano

Coarse salt and freshly ground black pepper

12 ounces tortilla chips

2 cups shredded cooked chicken

10 ounces Monterey Jack cheese, shredded

16 ounces salsa, store-bought or Salsa Verde (recipe follows)

1 avocado, pitted, peeled, and coarsely chopped

1 jalapeño, thinly sliced

Sour cream, for serving

1 Preheat the oven to 350°F with the rack in the middle position. Heat the safflower oil in a 10-inch skillet over medium-high heat. Add the onions and sauté until translucent, about 3 minutes. Add the black beans, cumin, and oregano. Season to taste with salt and pepper. Remove from the heat.

2 Arrange one-third of the tortilla chips on a baking sheet or oven-safe platter. Top with one-third each of the black beans, chicken, cheese, and salsa. Repeat this layering twice more. Transfer to the oven and bake until the cheese is melted throughout, 18 to 20 minutes. Remove from the oven and top with the avocado, jalapeño, and dollops of sour cream. Serve immediately.

salsa verde

makes 2 cups

½ white onion, coarsely chopped

2 garlic cloves, peeled

2 serrano or jalapeño chilies, stems removed

12 whole tomatillos

2 teaspoons salt

Peel the tomatillos and simmer in water for 5 minutes. Drain and roughly pulse in a blender or food processor with all other ingredients until smooth, adding water as necessary for desired consistency.

NOTES TO A NOVICE: ISN'T IT OBVIOUS?

A friend who can cook asked me incredulously why anyone would ever need a recipe for nachos. Isn't it obvious? she said. Observing my third son (who I thought had become an intermediate cook!) make nachos made me realize he still had a lot to learn about the basics.

Read (and reread!) the entire recipe before starting—including the ingredients list. Before you pour the can of black beans into the pan of cooked onions, it's important to know that the beans should have been drained first. If you didn't, use a slotted spoon to retrieve the actual beans and onions from the pan—mistakes can usually be fixed.

When a recipe calls for safflower oil, plain vegetable or canola oil is okay, too.

When a recipe calls for grated cheese, use a box grater. Set the grater firmly on the counter, rather than awkwardly holding it over the tray of tortilla chips. Also, remember that packaged grated cheese is much more expensive than the cheese you grate yourself.

While this may seem obvious to some, if you are using an oven, make sure the pan is oven-safe (and not an antique china platter).

If you want to use more cheese than the recipe calls for, go for it. Because nachos are layered, think about the quantities of ingredients in each layer. Remember, the whole dish has to heat through evenly in the oven to ensure melty cheese in every bite.

Read the cheese package, the outside of a can, and the label on the jar of salsa to learn the volume measure (ounces) of the container. No need to dirty a measuring cup if the measured amount can be deduced by what's written on the container. Absolute precision is not important for nachos—which makes this a perfect dish for an anxious cook to make.

If the recipe calls for shredded chicken, it is totally okay to use leftover cooked, shredded pork or sautéed ground meat. In fact, I applaud you for making smart use of your extra meat!

Clean up the kitchen as you go. No exceptions.

plain roast chicken

serves 4 to 6

One of the most frequently asked questions I receive from family and friends is how to make a simple roast chicken. (Truth be told, ever since I discovered the speed and ease of flat roasting chicken, page 52, I've practically forsaken the old-school whole roast chicken. But more about this later.) When roasting a chicken, the most important ingredient is salt. And, of course, you need an oven. If you have some aromatics, such as garlic, onions, or herbs, to stuff inside the bird, go for it, if you want. I don't truss or close the legs because I like as much surface skin area as possible cooked to a golden, crispy brown. Lifting the bird off the cooking surface (as described below) also allows more of the skin to golden up during cooking.

One 3- to 4-pound chicken, at room temperature

Coarse salt

1 lemon, poked all over with a fork (optional)

1 onion, cut into ½-inch-thick slices, or four or five ½-inch-thick slices bread

Extra-virgin olive oil or vegetable oil

1 Preheat the oven to 450°F with the rack in the middle position. Thoroughly pat dry the chicken with a paper or cloth towel. Generously salt the inside of the cavity. Stuff the lemon, if using, and 1 onion slice into the cavity. If there is a bag in the cavity with the innards, remove them from the plastic bag and stuff them back inside the bird.

2 Lay the onion or bread slices in one layer in a roasting pan or large skillet, making sure the chicken will fit on top of them with very little overlap. (Alternatively, use a roasting rack.) Rub oil on all sides of the bird and generously season the outside all over with salt. Place the chicken, breast side up, on the sliced onion or bread platform.

3 Pour a cup of water into the pan and transfer it to the preheated oven. The chicken is done when it is golden brown and cooked through, about 1 hour. An instant-read thermometer inserted into the thickest part and not touching bone should read 160°F (don't worry—the carryover heat will bring it to 165°F). The juices should run clear, not pink.

3 Transfer the bird to a cutting board, lightly tent with foil, and let rest for 10 to 15 minutes. Carve the chicken, place on a platter, and drizzle the pan juices over top.

BALANCING ACT

To add potatoes to this meal, place halved new potatoes or cubed Idaho potatoes on a baking sheet. Scatter some fresh herbs (such as thyme, rosemary, sage, or oregano) around the potatoes, if you like, and drizzle them with olive oil. Sprinkle with salt and a few grindings of pepper. Toss them to fully coat with oil and seasonings and put in the oven on the rack under the chicken during the last 40 minutes of the chicken's cooking time. Flip the potatoes halfway through their cooking time.

flat roast citrus chicken

serves 4

Flat roasting, also known as spatchcocking, is when a whole chicken has its backbone removed so that it can lie flat while cooking, giving you a roast chicken in about half the time it takes for a whole bird to cook. Finally (what took us so long?!), my husband discovered that you don't need to remove the whole bone before cooking. Simply cut along one side of the backbone with kitchen shears, leaving it attached on the other side—you can still flatten the bird, and though it may not look as pretty, the remaining backbone becomes a coveted treat for folks who love crispy skin and crunchy bones. *Photo on page 42.*

One 3-pound chicken, at room temperature

1 lemon or lime, thinly sliced and each slice quartered

1 orange or tangerine, thinly sliced and each slice quartered

Coarse salt and freshly ground black pepper

1 tablespoon extra-virgin olive oil

2 tablespoons unsalted butter

⅓ cup pitted green or black olives, halved

⅓ cup currants or raisins

4 to 6 garlic cloves, smashed and peeled

¾ cup chicken broth

1 Using kitchen shears, cut along one side of the backbone. Place the bird skin side up, and press down firmly to slightly flatten. Using your fingers, carefully separate the skin from the flesh (keeping it attached) where possible, taking care not to tear the skin. Slide some citrus pieces underneath the skin. (Use a chopstick or similar tool to shove the citrus into the legs and thighs.) Pat the chicken dry all over with paper towels. Season with salt and pepper generously on both sides.

2 Preheat the oven to 425°F. Heat a large, oven-safe skillet (such as a shallow, enameled cast-iron brazier) over high heat. Add the oil and 1 tablespoon of the butter and heat until the butter melts (it should bubble but not burn). Immediately add the chicken, skin side down. Cook without moving it, for 3 minutes. Turn the chicken over, taking care not to break the skin. Scatter the olives, currants, garlic, and any remaining citrus pieces around the chicken. Pour in the broth.

3 Transfer the skillet to the oven. The chicken is done when it is golden brown and cooked through, 40 to 45 minutes. An instant-read thermometer inserted into the thickest part and not touching bone should read 165°F. Transfer the chicken to a cutting board to rest for 10 minutes. Add the remaining 1 tablespoon butter to the pan drippings and swirl around to make a sauce.

4 Cut the chicken into pieces and serve with the pan sauce drizzled over top.

GET A SHALLOW BRAISING PAN

A good braising pan is lower than a Dutch oven but deeper than a sauté pan. It is a true multi-use pan sure to become a kitchen essential because you can brown, braise, poach, simmer, sauté, and even bake in it. In our house, we have a 3½-quart and a 5-quart braising pan, which are both used constantly. You will use it daily. Invest in a good one, like a Le Creuset made from enameled cast iron.

FLAT ROAST CHICKEN RIFFS

Tangy: season the bird on both sides with salt (plenty of it) and pepper. Cook as directed. Swirl some fresh lemon juice and butter into the pan drippings at the end.

Earthy: add paprika to the salt-and-pepper mix to burnish the bird with an auburn hue. Cook as directed.

Spicy: mix a teaspoon of garam masala (an Indian spice mix) with the salt and pepper, adding a little more salt than usual to balance the sweet spices. Cook as directed.

Garlicky: after browning the bird on the skin side, flip it over and snuggle several smashed garlic cloves under the carcass (instead of the citrus). They will lightly perfume the bird and enhance the flavor of the pan juices. Add a few sprigs of fresh herbs to the garlic pile, such as rosemary, sage, or oregano.

BBQ-y: generously season the bird on both sides with salt and pepper. Set up the grill for indirect heat (see page 10). Place the chicken skin side up on the side without fire. Cover the grill and open the vents. Cook for 45 minutes. Brush with your favorite barbecue sauce. Turn the bird over onto the fire side of the grill to crisp the skin (taking care not to burn), about 5 minutes. Brush sauce on the underside of the bird and flip to cook underside for 1 minute. Let rest for 10 minutes before cutting. Serve with extra barbecue sauce.

hot and crispy fried chicken

serves 4

Here's a unique method sure to satisfy your cravings for fried chicken when you're short on time (or energy). It's so satisfying that you may never again buy buttermilk to marinate chicken for frying the old-fashioned way. In this recipe, a spicy lemon marinade sets off a coating made from flour, cornmeal, and Parmesan cheese for a super delicious and quick-to-execute fried chicken. For best results, take the chicken out of the fridge at least 30 minutes before breading. Otherwise, the chicken will struggle to reach the frying temperature and the chill will create unwanted steam that will fight against crisping the skin.

½ cup lemon juice (from 2 to 3 lemons)

3 teaspoons coarse salt

1 teaspoon hot sauce

One 3-pound chicken, cut into serving pieces, breasts halved

⅓ cup all-purpose flour

⅓ cup cornmeal

2 tablespoons grated Parmesan or Romano cheese

½ teaspoon finely grated lemon zest

¼ teaspoon dried herb, such as oregano, thyme, or rosemary

1 cup vegetable oil

1 In a large bowl, combine the lemon juice, 1½ teaspoons of the salt, and the hot sauce. Add the chicken and marinate for up to 1 hour. Meanwhile, in a shallow dish, mix together the flour, cornmeal, Parmesan, remaining 1½ teaspoons salt, lemon zest, and dried herb. Dredge the marinated chicken pieces in the mixture until fully coated.

2 Heat the oil in a large skillet to 350°F. You can test the oil by dropping in a small piece of chicken skin—it should bubble immediately. Add the chicken pieces, skin side down, and cook, without moving, for 15 minutes (work in batches if necessary). Reduce the heat if the pan gets too hot or smoky while frying. Turn and cook on the other side until golden-crispy on the outside and tender on the inside, about 15 minutes. Drain on paper towels and serve.

FRIED CHICKEN MAGIC

For a Mexican flavor, use dried oregano and lime instead of lemon. Substitute añejo or cotija cheese for the Parmesan.

For chicken fingers, use boneless, skinless breasts or thighs cut into 1-inch-wide strips. Marinate, season, and coat as directed. Fry for 15 minutes total or oven-fry at 425°F for 20 minutes.

NOTES TO A NOVICE: HIGH HEAT

New cooks need to understand the importance of modulating the heat. Aggressive fire at the wrong time, with the wrong pan, or with the wrong ingredients can cause the food to crash and burn. At times, it's torture for me to watch my husband cook, as he thinks nothing of placing the pan on the burner, cranking up the heat, and moving on to other tasks (even as the kitchen fills up with an acrid burning-pan smell). The right flame at the right time means sugars will caramelize, fillets will brown, and skins will crust up. This is an essential part of cooking, but many recipes don't exactly explain it in the instructions.

Try to imagine taming the flame from the top on down. Get your pan extra hot (but unlike my husband, please pay constant attention), then turn the regulator knob down to control the temperature. Slowly heating your pan, especially with food in it, will not give you control. For example, a steak will never sear to your liking if you start it on a low heat. Its juices will seep out, the meat will steam rather than sear, and ultimately you will be disappointed in your meal. You need to hear a crazy sizzle when your steak first makes contact with the heat.

Whether making steak, chicken, or pork, it is best if you start with the protein at room temperature. Don't be afraid to take the meat out of the fridge up to two hours before cooking. Pat it dry with a paper towel to remove any residual moisture. You want the meat's surface to be dry when it hits the hot pan so that it instantly begins to form a crust. If you learn to understand your heat, you will become more confident cooking in a pan where the surface isn't coated with a nonstick material. (I am never quite sure how safe the so-called nonstick coating du jour is!)

When a recipe calls for browning a chicken, you must leave it undisturbed in the hot pan to create a firm, sealed skin. A well-browned skin will retract from the pan after several minutes and can be lifted more easily or moved around. You may be tempted to grab a fork or tongs and start pushing the chicken around to encourage browning, but wait—it will stick at this point. Have patience. There will be plenty of time later, when both sides have had adequate contact with the high heat.

Vegetables Love High Heat Too!

It's a wonder it took us so long to discover the riches of oven-roasted vegetables. In my childhood, nothing was nastier than the overboiled cauliflower and bungled Brussels sprouts we ate. The roasted-vegetable revolution had yet to happen in the 1970s household of my youth. In fact, it wasn't until the 1990s that we understood how high-heat roasting could transform cauliflower from a mushy white misfit into a hot vegetable version of a potato chip. Now we regularly roast two heads of sliced cauliflower at a clip for our five-folk-family dinners. Whether you're searing a steak, browning your bird, or coaxing the charm from a cruciferous vegetable, high heat is your cooking friend, as long as it is properly monitored.

roasted cauliflower

Cook this while your roast chicken is resting and your oven is still hot! Preheat the oven to 400°F. Core the cauliflower and cut it into ¼-inch-thick slices. It will crumble naturally but the slices usually stay mostly whole. Coat with olive oil and season with salt, spread out on a baking sheet, and roast for 20 to 30 minutes.

This high-heat method also works for Brussels sprouts. There are people who will tell you there is no way they'd eat a Brussels sprout—usually folks of a certain age who were raised on sulfurous, mushy green balls. Today, Brussels sprouts are the poster children for hip vegetables, street cred that they earned with a little high heat, olive oil, and salt.

honey mustard—glazed wings

serves 4

As far as I am concerned, ultimate chicken satisfaction is found in crunchy wing tips, that close-to-the bone meat roasted here in a double-whammy, zippy, salty-sweet combination. Add a couple of tablespoons of hot sauce for a spicy version.

2 pounds chicken wings, separated at the joints

1 tablespoon vegetable oil

2 teaspoons coarse salt

¼ cup Dijon mustard

¼ cup honey

¼ teaspoon ground white pepper

1 Preheat the oven to 375°F, with the rack in the center position. In a bowl, toss the wings with the oil and salt and transfer to a baking sheet, spreading them out for even baking. Bake for 30 minutes.

2 In a small bowl, combine the mustard, honey, and white pepper. Brush the wings with the glaze. Return the wings to the oven and continue baking for 15 minutes, turning and glazing the wings a few times. Increase the heat to 400°F and bake until golden, about 10 minutes more. Serve hot from the oven or at room temperature.

cacciatore

serves 6

This is one of our regular go-to dinners. Many variations exist, but this Italian chicken cacciatore has its roots in simple rustic cooking (it's what the hunter brought home to cook). You can leave out the mushrooms, use oregano instead of rosemary, and swap red wine for the white—in other words, this recipe is happily forgiving, developed over the generations as cooks made do with what was at hand.

One 3- to 4-pound chicken, cut into pieces (see tip on page 45), back, neck, and wing tips reserved for stock or soup

Coarse salt and freshly ground black pepper

¼ cup extra-virgin olive oil

2 strips bacon or 2 ounces pancetta, chopped

1 onion, chopped

2 garlic cloves, minced

2 teaspoons chopped fresh rosemary, or 1 tablespoon dried

10 ounces cremini or white button mushrooms, sliced (optional)

¾ cup white wine

1 cup chicken broth, or as needed

One 28-ounce can whole tomatoes, cut with scissors or lightly pulsed in a blender

1 Season the chicken generously with salt and pepper. Heat a large brazier pan or deep skillet over medium-high heat. Swirl in the oil. When it shimmers, work in batches to brown the chicken on both sides, starting skin side down, 3 to 4 minutes per side. Transfer to a plate.

2 Add the bacon, onion, garlic, and rosemary to the pan and cook until the bacon fat starts to render, 3 to 4 minutes. Discard the excess fat. Continue cooking (add the mushrooms if using) for an additional 3 minutes. Return the browned chicken to the pan. Raise the heat to high and add the wine, stirring to deglaze the pan and scrape up the browned bits on the bottom. Cook until most of the wine has evaporated, about 3 minutes.

3 Add the broth and tomatoes. Reduce the heat to a simmer, partially cover, and cook, stirring occasionally, until the chicken is tender and cooked through, 40 to 45 minutes. Remove the lid during the last few minutes of cooking to let the sauce thicken. Season to taste.

spicy chicken and chickpeas

serves 4 to 6

This recipe was sent to me several years ago by an awesome home cook from Texas. It has fabulous flavor and is cooked in a single pan, a treasured timesaving technique. Protein-rich chickpeas stretch the volume of this one-chicken dish even as they take on the delicious chicken-and-spice flavorings. Fresh cilantro enhances the Spanish flavor—parsley is a great option too.

⅓ cup extra-virgin olive oil

4 garlic cloves, smashed and peeled

½ cup chopped fresh cilantro or parsley leaves, plus more for garnish

2 tablespoons hot or sweet paprika, or up to 1 teaspoon smoked (or a combination)

1 teaspoon ground cumin

½ teaspoon crushed red pepper flakes

2 tablespoons coarse salt

1 teaspoon freshly ground black pepper

One 3-pound chicken, cut into serving pieces, breast pieces cut in half crosswise

Two 15-ounce cans chickpeas or white beans, drained

2 pints cherry or grape tomatoes

1 Mix together the oil, garlic, cilantro, paprika, cumin, red pepper flakes, salt, and pepper in a bowl. Transfer the marinade to zip-top bags or a large container suitable for marinating and add the chicken, chickpeas, and tomatoes, ensuring that everything, especially the chicken, is evenly coated with the marinade. Marinate in the refrigerator for a few hours, all day, or overnight.

2 When ready to cook, preheat the oven to 450°F. Dump the chicken and other ingredients, including any marinade, into a large roasting pan. Roast until the chicken is cooked through and browned and the tomatoes have burst and caramelized, about 30 minutes.

ABOUT PAPRIKA

This recipe lends itself to whatever paprika you choose to use, but here's a general word of caution on the subject: Sweet paprika is an excellent addition to any spice mix, as it adds both a lightly toasted mild pepper flavor and a beautiful orange tone. Hot paprika is spicy, but not ridiculously so. Smoked paprika, also known as pimentón, is an entirely different animal! It is strong, so a little goes a long way, and its flavor will totally permeate whatever you're cooking. Sometimes that is what you want, but more often than not, it should be used with discretion. You want it to round out the dish, not overpower it.

arroz con pollo

serves 4 to 6

This is a must in your repertoire, especially if you're clueless about how many people will be at your dinner table. I can't tell you how many times I find myself in this situation. A son or two brings home a friend or two, and the next thing I know every grain of rice has been scarfed up. The rice is infused with a delicious chicken flavor, so it'll stretch one bird into a truly bountiful and satisfying meal. If the dinner crowd is small, it reheats beautifully as leftovers. It's no wonder there are so many versions of it throughout Spain, Latin America, and the Caribbean. Nothing could be as easy to make, delicious, and universally satisfying as this one-pot dish. All you really need is some fat, chicken, salt, rice, and liquid, then just layer in any other extra ingredients that you might have on hand. Don't be afraid to cook it a little longer if the rice is still too moist after 40 minutes.

One 3- to 4-pound chicken, cut into 16 pieces (see opposite)

2 teaspoons coarse salt

Freshly ground black pepper

Extra-virgin olive oil

1 onion, finely chopped

4 garlic cloves, minced

2 small carrots, chopped

2 small celery stalks, chopped

½ green bell pepper, seeded and chopped

1 teaspoon ground cumin

3 cups white or brown rice

½ cup pimento-stuffed green olives, sliced

⅓ cup chopped fresh cilantro leaves, plus more for serving

5 cups chicken broth or water

1 Season the chicken pieces all over with 1 teaspoon of the salt and black pepper. Heat a large skillet (or two smaller ones, or cook in batches) over high heat. Swirl in enough oil to coat the bottom of the skillet. When the oil shimmers, place the chicken in the skillet, skin side down; you should hear an immediate sizzle. (Don't crowd the chicken in the pan—keeping space around each piece will ensure that the meat browns instead of steaming.) Don't move the chicken pieces; it takes a couple of minutes to sear the chicken so it doesn't stick. Brown on all sides, about 10 minutes per batch. Regulate the heat so it stays high but does not burn the meat. Remove the chicken from the pan.

2 Add the onions, garlic, carrots, celery, and bell pepper to the skillet. Sauté until the onion is translucent, 3 to 4 minutes, adding the cumin and remaining 1 teaspoon salt in the last few minutes. Add the rice, stirring to combine it completely with the vegetables. Stir in the olives and cilantro.

3 Pour in the broth. Nestle the chicken pieces around the skillet, amid the rice. Bring to a boil and then reduce the heat to a simmer. Cover and cook until the chicken is tender and the rice is cooked through, about 40 minutes (add 15 minutes if using brown rice).

budin azteca

serves 4 to 6

Over the decades, chunks (years!) of my cooking time have been devoted to learning new cuisines. My family says that authentic Mexican cooking got about five straight years of my attention. During that time, all my husband ever wanted for his birthday was a casserole-type dish called Budin Azteca: homemade tortillas layered with roasted and peeled peppers and freshly poached chicken. Here is a simplified version, using store-bought tortillas. I like to serve salad on top.

2 large poblano peppers

Ten 6-inch corn tortillas

4 tablespoons extra-virgin olive oil

1 small yellow onion, chopped

3 garlic cloves, minced

2 teaspoons coarse salt

2 tablespoons chopped fresh oregano leaves, or 1 tablespoon dried

2 teaspoons finely chopped chipotle chilies in adobo sauce

One 28-ounce can whole tomatoes and their juices, puréed roughly

1 cup heavy cream

1 pound chicken breast, poached and shredded (see opposite)

8 ounces Monterey Jack cheese, shredded

1 bunch radishes, thinly sliced

1 head romaine lettuce, thinly sliced crosswise

2 tablespoons white wine vinegar

1 Preheat the oven to 375°F, with the rack in the middle position. Char the poblanos over an open flame until blackened all over, about 5 minutes (see opposite). Char the tortillas over an open flame, turning once, 15 to 20 seconds per side, and stack and wrap in a clean kitchen towel to steam and soften. Peel the charred skins from the poblanos, discard the stems and seeds, and coarsely chop.

2 Heat 2 tablespoons of the oil in a medium sauté pan over medium-high heat. When the oil shimmers, add the onions and cook until translucent, about 3 minutes. Add the garlic, 1 teaspoon salt, oregano, and chipotles to the pan and cook for 30 seconds. Add the puréed tomatoes and simmer, stirring occasionally, until the sauce thickens slightly, about 10 minutes.

3 Spread 1 cup of the tomato sauce across the bottom of a 9-by-13-inch baking dish. Arrange 5 tortillas over the sauce, overlapping as needed, and cover with half the remaining sauce, half the poblanos, half the cream, half the chicken, and half the cheese. Repeat with the remaining tortillas, sauce, poblanos, cream, chicken, and cheese to make a second layer. Cover the baking dish with foil and bake for 30 minutes. Uncover and continue baking until bubbly and golden brown, about 15 minutes.

4 In a large bowl, combine the radishes, romaine, vinegar, and the remaining 2 tablespoons oil and 1 teaspoon salt. Serve each piece of the budin topped with a scoop of salad.

HOW TO POACH CHICKEN

Once you realize how easy it is to poach chicken breasts, you'll never be without them. They make a great addition to salads, soups, tacos, and casseroles.

Put 1 or 2 chicken breasts (or more) in a small saucepan, cover with chicken broth or water by 2 inches, and add one or more aromatics, such as onion, garlic, carrot, celery, black peppercorns, and bay leaf. Cover and bring to a gentle boil, then reduce the heat to a simmer and cook until just cooked through, 12 to 15 minutes (an instant-read thermometer, inserted into the thickest part of the breast, should register 160°F). Cool the chicken completely in the poaching liquid (if you used chicken broth, strain it and reserve for another use). Slice or shred the chicken to use immediately, or store the whole breasts in the refrigerator in a resealable plastic bag for up to 2 days. The poached breasts will keep in a freezer, well wrapped, for 6 weeks.

HOW TO ROAST A PEPPER

Jarred roasted red peppers are convenient—and worthy on many occasions—but there is no denying how good the home-roasted versions are, or that your kitchen will smell like a wood-fired restaurant when you roast a few. Prepare them this way and they can be scrambled into eggs, fried with potatoes (page 177), added to a pasta sauce, or used as a snack on top of toast.

If you have a gas stove, turn the burner flame to high, grip the stem end of the pepper with tongs and set the pepper directly on the flame, turning it often so that all sides char. This will take 5 to 8 minutes. Place the charred pepper(s) in a plastic bag. Close the bag and let the peppers steam in the bag for 10 to 15 minutes, which will make them easy to peel.

If your stove is electric, preheat the broiler. Slice the peppers in half lengthwise and place them on a baking sheet, cut sides down. Broil until the skin is dark and blistered, about 10 minutes. Cover with foil or put the peppers in a plastic bag as previously instructed.

When the peppers are cool enough to handle, rub off the charred skin and discard the seeds and ribs. (I don't rinse the peppers to remove the small charred bits, because I think that removes precious flavor.) Slice into strips and use as desired.

francese-style chicken

serves 4

Eggs and cheese combine in this dish to create a delicate, savory coating for the chicken breast, which also absorbs the lemon-wine-butter sauce. I love to serve this over a bed of capellini pasta, as one might find in an Italian-American restaurant, with Pizza Parlor Salad (page 196) or a simple steamed green vegetable, like Broccoli Two-Step (page 145), on the side.

2 large eggs, beaten

½ cup grated Parmesan or Romano cheese

1½ pounds boneless, skinless chicken breasts (about 4 pieces), pounded to slightly flatten

Coarse salt

2 tablespoons flour (Wondra is best for this)

¼ cup extra-virgin olive oil

1 tablespoon capers, rinsed

1 cup white wine

2 tablespoons unsalted butter

Finely grated zest and juice of 1 lemon

Chopped fresh parsley leaves, for serving (optional)

1. In a shallow dish, whisk together the eggs and the cheese. Season the chicken all over with salt and lightly coat it with flour. Dip each piece in the egg mixture to fully coat both sides.

2. Heat a large skillet over high heat. Swirl in the oil. When it shimmers, add the chicken pieces in a single layer, without crowding the pan (cook in batches if necessary). Sauté the chicken, cooking it through to a light golden color, for 2 minutes per side. Transfer to a plate.

3. Add the capers to the pan. Pour in the wine, and swirl it around the pan. Let it bubble away to cook off the alcohol and reduce its volume by half. Add the butter, swirling the pan as it melts. Stir in the lemon zest and juice. Remove the pan from the heat. Return the chicken to the pan and turn to coat with the sauce. Top with a spoonful of sauce and parsley, if desired, and serve.

HOW TO MAKE PAN SAUCE

Any time you cook a few pieces of seasoned protein like chicken, pork, beef, or fish in a sauté pan, use the flavor bits left behind in the pan (called fond) to make a sauce. Once the cutlet (or other protein) is cooked, remove it from the pan. (If too much fat is left behind, pour some—not all—off before proceeding.) Whisk in a dollop of something slightly savory and thick, like mustard, tomato paste, horseradish, or miso paste. Next, pour in ½ to 1 cup liquid, such as broth, wine, beer, or juice, and let it bubble away a little until slightly thickened. Pour the sauce over before serving.

coq au vin casserole

serves 6 to 8

I like to take classic dishes, such as the iconic French braise called coq au vin, and switch them up into a different format. A classic endures because of enticing flavor combinations. Here I'm sticking with the original idea (stew) and placing it in a different setting (casserole). If you have a deep, oven-safe skillet, the casserole may be cooked on the stovetop and transferred directly to the oven in the same pan.

1 tablespoon extra-virgin olive oil, plus more for drizzling

2 strips bacon, sliced crosswise

2½ pounds boneless, skin-on chicken thighs

Coarse salt and freshly ground black pepper

1 small onion, halved and thinly sliced

10 ounces white button mushrooms, quartered

3 tablespoons tomato paste

½ cup white wine

⅓ cup all-purpose flour

1½ cups chicken broth

1 pound extra-wide egg noodles, cooked 2 minutes less than instructed on package

2 cups shredded Muenster cheese

1 cup panko bread crumbs or regular dry bread crumbs

Pinch of paprika

1 Preheat the oven to 375°F. Heat a large skillet over medium-high heat. Swirl in the oil, add the bacon, and cook until the bacon is golden, 2 to 3 minutes. Remove the bacon from the skillet.

2 Season the chicken all over with salt and pepper. Add to the skillet and brown on both sides, about 4 minutes total. Transfer to a plate. Add the onions and mushrooms to the skillet, sautéing until golden brown, 5 to 8 minutes. Stir in the tomato paste. Deglaze the pan with the white wine, scraping up the browned bits on the bottom of the pan, until the wine has almost evaporated. Stir in the flour. Add the broth and stir to combine. Return the chicken and bacon to the skillet. Stir in the noodles and cheese.

3 Transfer the mixture to a greased 9-by-13-inch baking dish. Top with the bread crumbs, sprinkle with paprika, and drizzle with olive oil. Bake until the chicken is cooked through and the cheese has fully melted, about 25 minutes.

CASSEROLES ARE COOL

Casseroles may seem old-fashioned and dorky, but you've got to love a recipe cooked and served in the same dish. In addition, there's a pretty good chance that every bite will contain a little bit of everything you want to eat: protein, vegetables, savory creaminess, a crunchy topping, and hopefully a noodle-carb of some sort. Other casseroles worthy of consideration include the Budin Azteca (page 64), Spicy Chicken and Chickpeas (page 61), Shepherd's Pie (page 38), Eggplant Parmesan (page 170), and Eggplant Rollatini (page 169).

duck breast a l'orange

serves 2 to 4

This classic old-school recipe is definitely a special-occasion meal. After the first time I showed Luca (my twenty-year-old son) how easy it is to make this, it became his go-to dress-to-impress dish. The scored breast starts skin side down in a cold pan, and the pan and meat slowly heat up together until the golden crust forms on the meat, then is flipped to finish cooking. Duck breasts are more available than ever in the market and could not be simpler to cook. They are less expensive than a good steak and deliver the same meaty satisfaction. Serve this with Princely Potatoes (page 182) for a swoon-worthy plate of food. If you want to take it down a notch, forget the glaze and start with step 2 for a plain but perfectly cooked duck breast.

¼ cup sugar

A squeeze of lemon juice

2 tablespoons sherry vinegar

2 teaspoons finely grated orange zest

1 cup freshly squeezed orange juice (from about 2 oranges)

¾ cup chicken broth

3 tablespoons minced shallot (1 good-sized shallot)

2 boneless duck breast halves (8 to 10 ounces each)

1 teaspoon coarse salt

¼ teaspoon freshly ground black pepper

1 Place the sugar and lemon juice in a medium saucepan and set over medium-high heat. Shake the pan a few times as the sugar begins to dissolve, then use a fork to gently move the sugar on the edges to the center of the pan. Continue stirring in this manner until the sugar is a deep amber color, about 4 minutes. Remove from the heat and carefully stir in the vinegar, orange zest and juice, broth, and shallots. Return to medium-high heat and boil, stirring occasionally, until reduced to ⅔ cup, 20 to 25 minutes.

2 Meanwhile, score the fat of the duck breasts with the tip of a knife in a crosshatch pattern to form 1-inch diamonds. Season the breasts all over with salt and pepper. Place the breasts, fat side down, in a medium skillet over medium-high heat. Cook, without moving, until the skin is crisp and golden brown, about 10 minutes. Flip and continue cooking to the desired doneness, about 8 minutes more for medium-rare (125°F). Allow the meat to rest for 10 minutes before slicing and serving. Pour the sauce over the sliced duck.

EGGS
ALL DAY LONG

OPPOSITE: Scrambled Eggs (page 77)

THE ALL-IMPORTANT EGG

Think back to your fond memories from childhood and eggs will be there somewhere: Maybe it's a picture of you as a baby, with remnants of scrambled eggs strewn across a high-chair tray (and perhaps in your hair). Maybe it's the first time you helped your mother or grandmother make a cake, and loved being given the incredibly grown-up task of cracking the eggs. Eggs are delicious, versatile, healthy, easy, and affordable (how many other foods can you say all that about?).

When I was growing up, my mom cooked fried eggs the way she liked them, and eventually, it became the style I like, too: the yolk is runny enough to sop up with toast, yet the white is cooked through, on both top and bottom, to a firm, not tough, texture. Her trick was to tip a teaspoon of water into the hot pan, then cover the pan—this steams the surface albumen (aka that clear goo) so that it cooks through, while the bottom of the egg sautés in the bubbling butter.

My friend also cooks her fried egg just the way her mom did, so the edges have a golden-brown crispy ring. Her memory includes using a generous amount of oil (not butter), cooking over high heat, and tilting the pan while constantly spooning the molten fat over the top of the egg as the bottom cooks. The more you cook eggs, the more a signature style will emerge based on simple techniques you develop along the way—techniques that will make a lasting impression on the people you cook for.

Eggs are the first meal that each of our three sons cooked for himself. Our eldest, Calder, says the first time he wanted to cook in the kitchen, his dad taught him to fry an egg. He remembers a silver pan and cracking an egg into the bubbling butter. He's made his eggs the same ever since. Our other two sons also have each their own egg-cooking quirks. Miles: fried over-easy yet well cooked. Luca: scrambled with cheese.

A full carton of eggs in the refrigerator will rock your daily home cooking, whether you're a novice or an expert cook. Eggs are an endless source of nourishment and enchantment. Eat one hard-boiled, and it's a perfectly proportioned parcel of protein, healthy fat, and flavor. Or separate the white from the yolk, and suddenly dozens of preparations are possible, from meringues to custards to sauces.

If you are an omelet lover, get yourself a small nonstick pan or a well-seasoned classic omelet pan. The beat-up, aluminum Bon Chef omelet pan I acquired in the 1970s is still my pan of choice today. It was a great investment. Never washed with soap, it wipes clean with a paper towel. Sometimes I scrub it with a little salt and some oil. (In fact, if I'd just escaped a burning building and was certain my kids, husband, and dog were all out safe, I'd run back in to rescue that pan!) Think of any omelet as a welcoming canvas for a variety of cooked or fresh ingredients. It can be made in the French style, gently wrapped around a filling like a fine eiderdown, or with ingredients mixed right into the eggs. However it is prepared, an omelet is the perfect solution for breakfast, lunch, or dinner.

And lest we forget, without eggs, pancakes lack shape and fluff; French toast would just be soggy bread; and soups like Chinese egg drop soup or Italian stracciatella aka Rag Soup (page 92) would just be cups of broth. Put a cooked egg on any leftover in the fridge and you have a whole new dish.

soccer breakfast

serves 4 to 6

Ours is a soccer household, so when the weekend rolls around (and the boys are home), we are up early watching the matches of our favorite English Premier league teams on television. (Allegiance? No unification here—we split between Arsenal and Liverpool.) I know this 50-minute "full English" (minus the blood sausage) sprint of cooking might sound like a lot, but it's worth it. Savory pork breakfast meats, caramelized tomato, mushrooms, onions, slightly sweet-sauced beans, and buttery runny egg yolks all converge on a single plate. Have all your prep done so you can start cooking about 30 minutes before kickoff, and you'll be sitting down with everyone else eating a hot meal when the game starts. (For more on how to do this, see opposite.)

8 pork sausage links, aka "bangers"

8 ounces sliced bacon

1½ tablespoons unsalted butter, plus more for toast

1 onion, cut into ¼-inch-thick slices

4 small plum tomatoes, halved lengthwise, or 2 large tomatoes, sliced ½ inch thick

8 ounces mushrooms, cleaned and halved, or sliced if large

One 13½-ounce can Heinz Beans in Tomato Sauce, or similar Brit-style beans in red sauce

6 large eggs

Coarse salt and freshly ground black pepper

6 slices bread, toasted

1 Place the sausages and bacon in a large skillet over high heat. Cook through until golden brown, turning a couple of times, 10 to 15 minutes. Transfer to a paper towel–lined plate to drain, and keep hot in a warm oven.

2 Pour off most of the fat from the pan, then add 1 tablespoon of the butter and melt over medium-high heat. Add the onions, tomatoes, and mushrooms so they lie in a single layer and cook, turning once, until cooked through, with golden brown edges in spots, 4 to 5 minutes per side. (Cook in batches or use two pans.) Transfer the vegetables to a plate and keep hot in a warm oven. (If your pan is large enough, push the vegetables to one side and cook the eggs on the other.)

3 Place the beans in a small pot over medium heat. Place the toast in the toaster. Put your serving plates in the warm oven.

4 Add the remaining ½ tablespoon butter to the skillet and swirl it to coat. Immediately crack the eggs into the skillet. Add 1 teaspoon water to the pan, reduce the heat to medium-low, cover, and cook until the whites are set, about 2 minutes.

5 Place an egg or two on each warm plate. Add a couple of pieces of bacon, a sausage or two, a piece of tomato, some onions, a few mushrooms, and a spoonful of beans. Season with salt and pepper. Butter the toast and serve.

BALANCING ACT

Pay attention to the cooking sequence so you can sit down and eat with everyone when the food is hot, instead of being the short-order cook. First, prep everything you plan on serving. If coffee or tea is part of the plan, get the coffee or tea leaves in the pot and ready the cups, milk, and sugar. Ditto juice and glasses. Stack the plates and heat them in a warm oven (about 200°F). Silverware and napkins should be on the coffee table in front of the game. Don't forget the jam, ketchup, HP sauce, and any other condiments you plan on serving. If you don't have a large skillet, the cooking can be done simultaneously in a couple of pans.

CLOCKWISE FROM TOP LEFT:
fried, scrambled, bloodshot one eye, and poached

a perfect fried egg every time

makes 1 egg

If you like your fried egg sunny-side up and completely tender—with a runny yolk but no crispy brown edges—this is the method for you. (If you *do* like crispy edges, see page 72.)

½ teaspoon unsalted butter

1 large egg

Coarse salt and freshly ground black pepper

Heat a small nonstick or well-seasoned cast-iron skillet over medium-high heat. Add the butter and swirl it to coat the skillet. Immediately crack the egg into the skillet. Add 1 teaspoon water to the pan (around the outside of the egg into the butter), cover, reduce the heat to medium-low, and cook for 1 minute. Remove the egg from the pan immediately. Season to taste with salt and pepper and serve at once.

CODDLED CURDS

scrambled eggs

serves 1

So many of us mindlessly scramble eggs without much thought to better-than-serviceable results. But if you want the ultimate delicate curd, take care with the whisking (not too much), the pan (hot, but not too hot), and the butter (melted and foamy, not smoky and burned). Keep your eyes on the cooking (don't overstir), and turn off the heat while the curds are still wet—the pan's residual heat will carry on the cooking once it's off the flame. Worth every step!

3 large eggs

¼ teaspoon coarse salt

1 tablespoon unsalted butter

1 teaspoon chopped chives (optional)

1 In a medium bowl, whisk together the eggs and salt.

2 Heat a medium nonstick sauté pan over medium-high heat and swirl in the butter.

When the butter has melted and the foam subsides, pour the eggs into the pan. When eggs begin to set along the edges, pull them to the center of the pan with a spatula and tilt the pan to draw any uncooked egg out. Turn the scrambled eggs over a few times until they are no longer runny but still wet. The entire cooking process will take less than 1 minute.

3 Transfer the eggs to a warm plate, sprinkle with chives, if you like, and serve.

bloodshot one eye

serves 2

Add some pepper strips to an egg-in-the-hole and you have a variation on my Italian grandmother's go-to breakfast. Not until I saw the movie *Moonstruck*, set in the Brooklyn brownstone kitchen of a multigenerational Italian family, did this recipe resurface from my memory—and find its spot in my own breakfast traditions. In the film, the matriarch stands over the stove making these eggs, and as I watched, my own memories locked in place. Leave out the peppers, and you have a plain old one eye.

2 slices white bread

1½ tablespoons unsalted butter

6 thin strips jarred roasted red pepper

2 large eggs

Coarse salt and freshly ground black pepper

1 Using a 2-inch round cookie cutter or a drinking glass, cut a hole in the center of each piece of bread. Heat a nonstick skillet over medium-high heat. Swirl in 1 tablespoon of the butter. Add the bread and the cutout rounds to the pan and cook to golden brown, about 2 minutes.

2 Drop a small dab of butter in each hole in the bread. Lay the pepper strips in the hole to resemble a "bloodshot" eye. Crack an egg into each hole over the peppers. Season with salt and pepper. Cook until set, about 1 minute. Carefully flip the egg-imbedded bread slice and the cutout rounds, and cook until fully set, about 1 minute more. Serve the bloodshot one eye on a plate, along with the toasted cutout rounds for dipping in the yolks.

LIVESAVER LESSON

A LOAF IN EVERY FREEZER

Toast makers, are you sick of running out of bread or seeing your bread go stale? Hello? Freezer alert! Always keep a loaf of sliced bread in there. Use a knife to separate as many frozen slices as you need and then pop them directly in the toaster. Stash a couple of varieties, if possible. I like to eat a sprouted whole-grain bread that no one in my family likes, so I stow it in the freezer to ensure that there is always a piece when I want it.

poached eggs

serves 1

If you are poaching just one egg, try whisking the simmering water into a whirlpool and then dropping the cracked egg into the center of that eddy. The centrifugal force will hold the white together. If you are serving poached eggs and want them all ready at the same time, make them up to 2 hours ahead of time and place them on a baking sheet lined with a clean cotton towel. (They are not as fragile as you might think.) Just before serving, submerge the cooked eggs in boiling water for 10 seconds to reheat.

Vinegar (optional)

2 large eggs

Fill a medium pot with water. Add a splash of vinegar, if you like, cover, and bring to a gentle boil. Break the eggs one at a time into a small cup and slip each into the water. Reduce the heat to a simmer and poach until the whites turn opaque and the yolks are encased but still soft and runny, 3 to 4 minutes. Use a slotted spoon to transfer the eggs to a plate. (I like to first place them on a cotton towel, to remove excess water.)

eggs benedict

Make a hollandaise: blend 4 egg yolks, the juice of 1 lemon, and a pinch of salt in a blender. With the motor running, slowly pour in 1½ sticks (12 tablespoons) melted butter to thicken. Top a toasted and buttered English muffin with a slice of ham, smoked salmon, or steamed spinach. Place a poached egg on top. Drizzle with the hollandaise sauce.

one-eyed french toast

serves 4

French toast embedded with a fried egg updates an old standby: the one-eye, aka eggs-on-a-raft. This version is a savory French toast topped with a runny egg yolk and sitting in a river of sweet maple syrup. So yes, it combines all the flavors and textures you crave when you think about breakfast. Add a salty-porky breakfast meat on the side for a full hearty meal.

6 large eggs

¼ cup milk

½ teaspoon pure vanilla extract

4 slices bread

1 tablespoon unsalted butter, plus more for serving

Coarse salt

Maple syrup, warmed

1 In an 8-inch square baking dish, whisk together 2 of the eggs, the milk, and vanilla extract. Using a 2-inch round cookie cutter or drinking glass, cut out a hole in the center of each of the bread slices. Add the slices of bread and cutout rounds to the egg mixture in a single layer and soak, turning occasionally, until the egg mixture is absorbed.

2 Heat a large nonstick skillet over medium heat. Swirl in 2 teaspoons of the butter. When it is bubbling, add the bread and bread rounds and cook until golden brown, about 2 minutes.

3 Drop a small dab of the remaining 1 teaspoon of butter in each hole in the bread. Crack an egg into each hole. Sprinkle a pinch of salt on each egg. Cook until set, about 1 minute. Carefully flip the egg-imbedded bread slice and the cutout rounds, and cook until the whites are set and the yolks are still runny, about 1 minute more.

4 Serve each slice with the cutout round on the side, slathered in butter and drizzled with warm maple syrup.

LIVESAVER LESSON

BAKE YOUR BACON

When you need to cook enough bacon for a crowd or for young men with big appetites, bake it. You'll have a hard time going back to the skillet. Here's how: Lay the strips flat on a straight-sided, foil-covered baking sheet. Bake at 400°F until golden brown and crispy, about 15 to 18 minutes. No need to turn the bacon during cooking, but lift the cooked strips from the fat and let them drain on paper towels or recycled paper grocery bags before serving.

soft-boiled eggs with toast

serves 1

The warm, runny yolk and softly gelled white of a soft-boiled egg, scooped out and combined with crisp, golden pieces of torn toast, is the pinnacle of comfort food.

2 large eggs, at room temperature (if straight from the fridge, place in warm water for 5 minutes)

2 slices bread

2 teaspoons unsalted butter

Coarse salt and freshly ground black pepper

1 Bring a saucepan of water to a boil. Gently lower the eggs into the pan using a slotted spoon and cook for 4 minutes. Remove and place briefly in cold water. Meanwhile, toast the bread and spread the slices with butter. Remove the eggs from the water, crack open the tops, and scoop the whites and yolks into a small bowl.

2 Break the buttered toast into pieces and add to the bowl. Sprinkle with salt and pepper. Stir the eggs and toast together just until the toast is coated with yolk.

WORTH KNOWING

HOW TO HARD BOIL EGGS

Put large eggs in a pot and cover with cold water by 1 inch. Bring to a boil; don't walk away and let them boil away unnoticed. As soon as the water boils, remove the pan from the heat, cover, and let it sit for 10 minutes. Drain the eggs and submerge them in cold water before peeling. The yolks will be just cooked, while the whites will be fully cooked without being rubbery.

banana baby

serves 2 to 4

A single, large puffy pancake is not only an easy way to serve multiple mouths at once, but it also makes quite a visual impression. This recipe is more custardy than cakey, and while it calls for bananas, other fruits—including sliced peaches, plums, apricots, pears, and apples—work well, too. Even without any fruit at all, it's perfectly scrumptious served with melted butter and sprinkled with powdered sugar.

4 large eggs, beaten

¾ cup whole milk

¾ cup all-purpose flour

¼ teaspoon coarse salt, plus more for sprinkling (optional)

3 teaspoons sugar, plus more for sprinkling (optional)

¼ teaspoon pure vanilla extract

3 tablespoons unsalted butter

2 ripe bananas, cut on the bias into ½-inch-thick slices

¼ teaspoon ground cinnamon, for sprinkling (optional)

Maple syrup or orange wedges, for serving

1 Preheat the oven to 425°F. Put a 9-inch skillet (preferably well-seasoned cast-iron or oven-safe nonstick) in the oven to heat up. Meanwhile, put the eggs, milk, flour, ¼ teaspoon of the salt, 1 teaspoon of the sugar, and the vanilla extract in a blender and blend until well combined and foamy, about 50 seconds. Alternatively, whisk the flour, sugar, and salt in a large bowl and make a well in the center. Add the eggs, milk, and vanilla extract and whisk until well combined. This can be done several hours ahead.

2 Transfer the skillet to the stovetop over medium-high heat and swirl in 2 tablespoons of the butter. Add the bananas to the pan and sprinkle the remaining 2 teaspoons sugar over them. Cook, without moving, until caramelized, about 1½ minutes. Using a long-handled spatula, carefully turn the bananas over. Pour the batter into the pan and immediately place the pan in the oven. Cook until the pancake is puffed, set, and golden brown on top, 15 to 18 minutes.

3 If using, whisk together the cinnamon, 1 teaspoon sugar, and ¼ teaspoon coarse salt and sprinkle over the pancake. Cut into quarters and serve with dots of the remaining butter and maple syrup or orange wedges.

A SAVORY SLANT

The Brits have a delicious savory baked dish called Toad in a Hole that is cooked similarly to my Banana Baby. Bangers (aka sausages) are fried first in the pan and then the same batter I use is poured over the sausages. The whole thing is baked at 425°F for 20 minutes and then served with a lusty mustard.

french toast with fresh strawberry jam

serves 4

Without the strawberry sauce, this is your basic French toast recipe—one that can be served slathered in butter and drizzled with maple syrup. Please don't be scared off by the prospect of making your own strawberry jam for this recipe; it can be made at home really quickly, which is exactly what you should do when strawberries are at their seasonal best.

2 pounds strawberries, hulled and quartered lengthwise, plus more for serving

¼ cup sugar

1 teaspoon coarse salt

½ teaspoon ground ginger (optional)

Finely grated zest and juice of 1 lime or lemon

6 large eggs

1¾ cups milk

½ teaspoon pure vanilla extract

8 slices of your favorite sturdy bread (day-old bread is best)

3 tablespoons unsalted butter, plus more for serving

1 Set aside 1 cup of the strawberries for garnish. Place the remaining berries in a medium saucepan and add the sugar, ½ teaspoon of the salt, the ginger, and lime zest and juice. Bring to a boil over medium-high heat, then reduce the heat and simmer, stirring occasionally, until the strawberries become very soft and the liquid is thick and syrupy, about 10 minutes. Remove the saucepan from the heat and let cool. The jam can be made ahead and refrigerated for up to 6 weeks.

2 Heat a griddle or large sauté pan over medium-high heat. In a large baking dish, whisk together the eggs, milk, vanilla extract, and remaining ½ teaspoon salt. Soak the bread in the egg mixture, flipping once, until it's soaked through but not mushy, about 1 minute per side. Melt the butter on the hot griddle and cook the bread, flipping once, until golden brown on both sides and crisp along the edges, 2 to 3 minutes per side.

3 Serve the French toast with a dab of butter, some strawberry jam, and garnished with the remaining fresh strawberries.

ABOUT STRAWBERRIES

Whether you buy them at the store or pick your own, strawberries are highly perishable and will not last if there is even one dented and squashed berry in the bunch. Choose ones that are evenly red and have dark green tops and a fresh berry aroma. Take a minute to go through each piece of fruit, and discard any bruised ones—as they decompose, they'll drag their neighboring berries down with them. Wash them only when you are ready to use them or they will perish more rapidly. Don't waste your money on inferior fresh berries—if you can't find primo fresh berries, buy flash-frozen unsweetened ones instead.

baked raisin bread french toast
with orange butter sauce

serves 6 to 8

The beauty of this dish is that you can prep it the night before and pop it in the oven in the morning, making it an ideal choice for a weekend filled with houseguests. You can serve the French toast with the suggested orange sauce, or skip it and just add a drizzle of honey or maple syrup instead. Make a platter of cooked sausages and Three Melon Salad (page 237), and it's a full-on brunch.

1 tablespoon unsalted butter, at room temperature

1 loaf raisin bread, sliced (about 1 pound)

6 large eggs

2 cups milk

½ teaspoon pure vanilla extract

⅓ cup plus 1 tablespoon sugar

1¼ teaspoons ground cinnamon

½ teaspoon coarse salt

THE ORANGE BUTTER SAUCE (OPTIONAL)

8 tablespoons (1 stick) unsalted butter

⅓ cup water

3 large egg yolks

⅓ cup sugar

1 tablespoon grated orange zest

¼ cup orange juice

1 Make the French toast: Butter the bottom and sides of a 2½-quart baking dish. Shingle the bread slices over the bottom of the baking dish. In a medium bowl, whisk together the eggs, milk, vanilla extract, ⅓ cup of the sugar, 1 teaspoon of the cinnamon, and the salt. Pour the egg mixture evenly over the bread slices. Cover the mixture with parchment paper or plastic wrap and press down gently until the liquid ingredients soak through the top of the bread. Cover the baking dish with foil and refrigerate for at least 8 hours or up to overnight.

2 Preheat the oven to 350°F, with the rack in the middle position. Remove the baking dish from the refrigerator and let it stand at room temperature for 30 minutes. Remove the foil and parchment.

3 In a small bowl, combine the remaining 1 tablespoon sugar and ¼ teaspoon cinnamon. Sprinkle evenly over the bread. Bake for 45 minutes or until the French toast is puffed and golden brown. Transfer to a cooling rack and let stand for 10 minutes.

4 Meanwhile, make the orange-butter sauce, if you like: Melt the butter with the water in a medium saucepan and bring to a simmer. In a medium bowl, whisk together the egg yolks and sugar. Slowly pour the butter mixture into the egg mixture, whisking continuously. Return the sauce to the saucepan and whisk in the orange zest and juice. Return the saucepan to the stovetop and cook over medium heat, whisking continuously, until thickened slightly, about 2 minutes. Spoon the warm sauce over the French toast and serve immediately.

LIVESAVER LESSON

MORE MAKE-AHEAD EGGY FAVORITES

You don't have to wake up at the crack of dawn to cook brunch. Egg and Ham Pie (page 90), for example, can be made completely ahead the night before, and then reheated in the oven at 200°F for 10 minutes before serving. Stratas are another type of brunch casserole, with savory layers of bread, cooked vegetables and/or meat, shredded cheese, and eggs (see *Mad Hungry Cravings*, page 36). They are assembled in advance, rest in the refrigerator overnight so the bread can soak up all the egg mixture, and bake in less than an hour in the morning.

open-faced vegetable omelet

serves 8

This open-faced omelet is one of those recipes to deploy at any time of the day or night. It's incredibly easy and versatile. Do you have many mouths to feed? Check. Have a carton of eggs in the fridge? Check. Need something quick and easy? Check. Need something meatless? Check. This omelet is for you! Cut into wedges and serve with toast. Use it as a sandwich filling for lunch (any kind of roll will do) or as part of a dinner on a cold winter night served with some fried sausages and Baked Sweet Potatoes (page 180).

2 tablespoons extra-virgin olive oil

1 medium onion, chopped

Coarse salt

1 tomato, cored and chopped

1 large bunch Swiss chard, ends trimmed, stems thinly sliced and leaves cut into 1-inch-long strips

¼ teaspoon freshly ground black pepper

12 large eggs

1 teaspoon hot sauce, such as Sriracha

3 to 4 ounces Cheddar cheese, shredded (about ¾ cup)

1 Preheat the broiler. Heat a 12-inch oven-safe nonstick or cast-iron pan over medium-high heat. Swirl in 1 tablespoon of the oil. When it shimmers, add the onion and season with salt. Sauté for 2 minutes. Add the tomato, stir, and cook for 1 minute. Add the Swiss chard and season with salt and the pepper. Cook for 5 minutes, then transfer to a plate.

2 Return the pan to medium-high heat. Swirl in the remaining 1 tablespoon oil. Crack the eggs into a bowl and add the hot sauce. Whisk the eggs together and pour into the pan. Allow the eggs to set a bit and then, using a spatula, pull the eggs away from the sides of the pan and allow the raw egg to flow underneath. Cook until the eggs are almost fully set. Spread the vegetables over the eggs and sprinkle the cheese on top. Transfer the pan to the broiler and broil until the cheese has melted and the eggs are cooked through, about 1 minute.

CRISPER CRASH

Feel free to improvise with this recipe, depending on what bits of veggies linger in the crisper. For example, spinach can be swapped for Swiss chard. Add a seeded and chopped green pepper. If you don't have a fresh tomato, a couple of chopped canned ones will work, or you can leave them out altogether. Instead of Cheddar, use whatever grating cheese you have on hand, such as Monterey Jack, Swiss, or Gouda. Are you catching my drift? You can use almost anything—and you cannot mess this up!

egg and ham pie

makes one 9-inch quiche

Please do not be deterred by the pie dough part of the recipe. This cream cheese dough is much easier to roll out and work with than a butter-based shortcrust, which is the dough of choice for classic French quiches. The cream cheese crust is tender and delectable—so what if it's not traditional? This dish only calls for half the recipe of pastry dough—make a second pie (feel free to riff on the filling) or freeze the other half for another day. You can make the pie ahead of time and reheat it in a 200°F oven for 10 minutes.

½ recipe Cream Cheese Pastry Dough (recipe follows)

2 cups grated Jarlsberg, Swiss, or Gruyère cheese

1 heaping cup diced ham

4 large eggs

2 cups half-and-half

½ teaspoon dry mustard or prepared Dijon mustard

½ teaspoon Worcestershire sauce

Couple dashes of hot sauce, such as Tabasco

Grated Parmesan cheese, for sprinkling

Pinch of freshly grated nutmeg

1. Preheat the oven to 400°F. Roll the pastry dough into a 10- to 11-inch disc and press into a pie pan. Cut off the overhanging pieces and crimp the edge using your thumbs and forefingers. Scatter the Jarlsberg cheese over the bottom, and top with the ham.

2. Whisk together the eggs, half-and-half, mustard, Worcestershire, and hot sauce in a bowl. Pour the mixture over the cheese and ham, stirring slightly to distribute the egg mixture through the cheese. Top with a little Parmesan and the grated nutmeg.

3. Bake for 40 minutes. Tent the top edges with foil if the crust browns too much before the eggs set. Let rest for at least 30 minutes before cutting and serving.

LET IT REST

After all the work you put into your pie, it's tempting to slice it into that golden, puffy, custard fresh out of the oven. Please resist. If you want a nice clean wedge, you must let the juices rest and the filling fully set—for at least 30 minutes (but preferably more). Otherwise, it'll dissolve into a puddle of mush before your eyes.

cream cheese pastry dough

makes enough dough for two 9- or 10-inch pies

This is, hands down, the most forgiving and easy pastry dough you'll ever use. As long as you're gathering the ingredients, you might as well make enough dough for more than one pie. If making just one, the dough can be frozen, well sealed, for up to 6 months.

8 tablespoons unsalted butter, at room temperature

4 ounces cream cheese, at room temperature

¼ cup heavy cream

1½ cups plus 2 tablespoons all-purpose flour, plus more for rolling out the dough

½ teaspoon coarse salt

1 Process the butter, cream cheese, and cream in a food processor, stand mixer, or by hand to thoroughly combine. Add the flour and salt. Process just until combined and the dough holds together in a ball. Turn the dough out onto a well-floured surface and divide into 2 pieces. Flatten into discs and wrap each in plastic wrap. Refrigerate for at least 30 minutes before rolling out. If the dough is chilled overnight, take it out 15 minutes before rolling out.

2 Rub flour on a rolling pin. Working with one disc of dough at a time, roll them out on a well-floured surface. Apply some pressure to the rolling pin and roll gently from the center of the dough to the top and bottom edges. Rotate the disc and roll to the top and bottom edges again. Re-flour the work surface and rolling pin, turn the dough over, and continue to roll the dough from the center out to the edges. Turn over and roll again, rotating the disc to ensure even rolling until the dough is about 12 inches in diameter, thin but not transparent.

rag soup

serves 4

This is my mom's favorite soup for two reasons: (1) it's ideal when a loved one is feeling sick, and (2) it's ideal when there is nothing else in the house to cook or eat. If you have a couple of boxes or cans of chicken broth in the pantry (or homemade broth in the freezer—see opposite), you are just a few ingredients away from a nourishing and delicious bowl of comfort.

1 quart chicken broth, homemade (see opposite) or store-bought

4 large eggs

⅓ cup grated Italian cheese, such as Pecorino Romano or Parmesan

1 tablespoon chopped fresh parsley leaves (optional)

Pinch of freshly ground black pepper

Handful of fresh spinach (optional)

Coarse salt

1 Bring the broth to a boil in a medium pot. Meanwhile, whisk together the eggs, cheese, parsley (if using), and pepper.

2 Slowly stir the egg mixture into the boiling broth. It will clump together in small "rags." Add the spinach (if using) and stir until wilted, about 2 minutes. Season to taste with salt. Serve immediately.

HOW TO MAKE A SIMPLE CHICKEN BROTH

It's inevitable. Maybe not today, but one day, you or someone you care about will feel lousy. For whatever reason, your child, parent, sibling, friend will stumble—whether physically or emotionally. During these times, it is important to stop and slow way, way down. Think hard about everything you put in your or your loved one's body. Choose your foods wisely.

A cup of strong chicken broth is one of the most powerful kitchen cures there is and an essential ingredient in any number of soups, stews, and braises. Use this "elixir" as a medicinal potion, especially if you catch the early signs of a cold and want to blast it right out of you. Practically since the dawn of time, chicken soup has been relied on to make us feel better when we ache and sniffle and take to our beds.

To make a good broth, buy a bunch of backs, drumsticks, or wings—any chicken parts that are mostly bone (not breasts unless the meat has been removed). Collect any random chicken parts, like the neck that comes inside a whole bird, in a resealable plastic bag and keep in your freezer until you're ready to make stock.

1. To begin, make the first infusion. Dump all the chicken parts in a pot, along with a cut-up onion and some smashed garlic cloves. Add a roughly chopped carrot, celery stalk, and a handful of parsley—whatever you have on hand is fine. Cover the chicken and vegetables with water (if you have a box of store-bought chicken broth, use it along with the water for added flavor). Bring the broth to a boil, reduce the heat, and simmer for 1 hour. Strain the broth, discard the solids, and return the liquid to the pot.

2. Reduce the broth to liquid gold, boiling it until it has reduced to half the original amount. Season with salt to taste. Drink a cup as hot as possible. Repeat throughout the day.

To make a fortified "elixir," add a whole head of garlic, cut in half, along with a handful of roughly chopped fresh ginger, 2 or 3 hot green chilies (use the tip of a knife to make a slit in each), and another handful of parsley or cilantro. Bring to a boil and simmer for about 20 minutes. Strain again, discard the solids, and return the broth to the pot.

THE SEAFOOD STORY

OPPOSITE: Tangy Grilled and Glazed Salmon (page 105)

FIGURING OUT FISH AND SAVORING SEAFOOD

Everywhere we turn, we're told to eat more fish because of the myriad health benefits attached to its long-chain fatty acids. But then we're told not to eat too much fish, due to mercury. Or, don't eat the *wrong* kind of fish, due to ocean ecosystem concerns. No wonder we're all left floundering when we see a piece of flounder in the fishmonger's case. Here is what to keep in mind when you shop:

Let the fish you choose determine the recipe you make. Otherwise you'll miss out on the opportunity to get the freshest, most seasonal, and affordable option of the day. Worse still, you may find yourself exhaustively hunting around for a variety called for in a recipe that is way too expensive, overfished, day-old, or unavailable. Would you really insist on having the defrosted, plastic-wrapped crabstick when you could have the fluke that you watched them bring in from the dock?

Talk to the purveyor. Whether you buy at a fish market or the fish counter of a supermarket, there's always someone who can answer a few basic questions. Ask what fish (if any) is abundant from local waters at that particular time. It's often the freshest and most affordable. If the fish is flown or trucked in from another area, find out where it came from and when. And many good fish options are flash frozen at sea (such as wild salmon), and can be of superior quality, too. They can be found in the freezer section or defrosted at the seafood counter. Decide for yourself, using these various criteria to determine freshness, cost, and sustainability.

Stare into the fish's eyes (but no, not in the romantic sense). They should be sparkling clear and devoid of a cloudy cataract look. If the fish is already cut, smell and touch it. Firm and unblemished is good (think: glistening snapper), mushy is bad (think: slimy tilapia). Fish should smell like the ocean, not fishy or like garbage or armpits. Raw fish is only smelly when it's on its way out.

Find out if the fish is farmed or wild. Wild is more expensive but is often a tastier choice. Eat the good stuff, just less of it. I dislike farmed salmon, which to me tastes like sawdust because of suspicious farming practices (the fish are raised in crowded pens of poorly circulated water). Even though both farmed and wild salmon have equal amounts of the good-for-you omega fat, farmed has twice as much unhealthy saturated fat. Every year, between June and September, wild Alaskan salmon is fresh, abundant, and delicious. Eat it then or choose flash-frozen wild Alaskan salmon and make Tangy Grilled and Glazed Salmon (page 105). Flash-frozen fish fillets, sold in reputable, quality supermarkets, are affordable and serviceable for weeknight dinners, especially if prepared flavorfully, like Haddock Italiano (page 102).

Of course, some farmed fish are on par with (or even better than) their free-swimming counterparts. Rainbow trout are farmed in raceways, which mimic a free-flowing river and use large amounts of fresh water. Arctic char (with a pink flesh that resembles trout) are a lesser known relative, and come from eco-friendly farms that conserve water and prevent water pollution. Fillets from both these varieties make an excellent choice for pan-sautéing, as in the quick-and-easy Trout with Almonds (page 98).

Care about this precious food resource. The fish supply in our oceans, lakes, and rivers is constantly changing. Some fish are presently endangered and others, like monkfish, have rebounded from depleted stocks. Diversification of the seafood we eat can be one of the most important tools to ensure sustainability. Get in the habit of consulting SeafoodWatch.org to determine if the fish available to you is a good choice. The more we all ask questions, the more our demand for information will urge answers.

If you need proof that these rules are effective, consider this anecdote, which took place when I visited my mom in Gloucester, Massachusetts, the oldest fishing village in America. Over the years of visiting (and cooking with) my mom, I'd struck up a relationship with a fishmonger who one day suggested I try a fish I'd never heard of—cusk, a member of the cod family. (As clichéd as it sounds, it's worth it to ask, "What's good today?" when you walk into a store.) She said it was the freshest fish of the day from local waters, and it also happened to be the least expensive option in the case. The fillet had firm-textured flesh and was somewhat oilier than other whitefish, so it would do well getting grilled, fried, or baked. The dense meat holds together nicely when cooked, which makes it ideal for soups, chowders, and kebabs. I bought it and was so happy with the results that I now grab it whenever it's available and have become much more adventurous in trying out other lesser-known fish. All this from a friendly chat with the fishmonger, whom I'd spent some time getting to know!

trout with almonds

serves 4

The mellowness of trout combined with this simple French technique make this a great entry-level fish dish for neophyte fish-eaters. The fillets cook quickly, and the browned butter imparts a mild, almost nutty flavor, which is why I like to pair the trout with toasted almonds. You can swap in any similarly thin, delicate fillet, such as sole, catfish, fluke, or black bass, and use pecans, hazelnuts, or cashews instead of almonds. Or omit the nuts if you want, and top each fillet with a wedge of lemon as an alternative. Serve with Small Steamed New Potatoes (page 175) and Barely Touched Spinach (page 161)—one of my favorite dainty meals (by my standards, anyhow).

½ cup sliced almonds

½ cup all-purpose flour

½ teaspoon coarse salt

¼ teaspoon cayenne pepper

1 cup milk

4 trout fillets

1 tablespoon extra-virgin olive oil

1 tablespoon unsalted butter

2 garlic cloves, smashed and peeled

1 Toast the almonds and set aside. Combine the flour, salt, and cayenne pepper in a flat dish. Pour the milk into another dish. Place the trout fillets in the milk and let sit for a couple of minutes.

2 Heat a large sauté pan over medium heat. Swirl in the oil and add the butter. Dredge both sides of the fillets in the flour mixture and add to the pan. Raise the heat, add the garlic cloves to the pan, and swirl them around. Flip the trout after 2 minutes and remove the garlic (you don't want it to brown). Cook until the fish is cooked through and lightly golden brown, 1 to 2 minutes more. Scatter the toasted almonds over the fish. Serve immediately.

WORTH KNOWING

HOW TO TOAST NUTS

Toasting nuts intensifies their flavor and crunches up the texture. Preheat the oven or toaster oven (for a small amount) to 350°F. Spread the nuts on a baking sheet in a single layer and put in the oven for 10 minutes, shaking the sheet several times. You can also heat a small, dry skillet over medium heat, add the nuts, and continue to turn them over until they are a light golden brown. Do not take your eyes off the toasting nuts—there is a very fine line between toasted and burned!

pan-seared red snapper with citrus herb relish

serves 2

There are entire schools of people who will state avowedly that they "do not like fish." But trust me, they can be won over (or at least learn to make exceptions) with healthy, refreshing recipes like this one: they will see the top first—a colorful, sweet relish that looks familiar and appealing—and then get a waft of its clean citrus-mint scent. A fresh, mild fish, sautéed until golden brown, will not seem "fishy" to a fish-phobe, and it becomes a protein platform underneath that tangy, citrusy salsa.

2 red snapper fillets, skin-on (about 1½ pounds), or other mild, semifirm white fish, such as yellowtail snapper, skate, or cod

1 orange, peeled and segmented into sections

1 pink grapefruit, peeled and segmented into sections

1 celery stalk, peeled and thinly sliced on the bias

1 tablespoon finely sliced fresh mint, plus more for serving

2 teaspoons chopped fresh chives

Coarse salt and freshly ground white pepper

2 teaspoons safflower or vegetable oil

1 Remove the fish from the refrigerator 15 minutes before cooking and let it come to room temperature. Thoroughly pat dry each fillet with paper towels. Carefully score the skin lightly with a sharp knife. Do not pierce the flesh.

2 Cut the orange and grapefruit segments into thirds. Place in a bowl with the celery and toss with the mint and chives.

3 Heat a 12-inch nonstick skillet over very high heat. Just before searing, season the flesh side of the fish with salt and pepper. Swirl in the oil and add the fillets, flesh sides down, to the pan. Sear for 2 minutes. Season the skin with salt and pepper and flip. Cook for 2 minutes more. Both sides should be golden brown and slightly crispy. Serve each fillet with a scoop of citrus relish on top. Garnish with fresh mint.

haddock italiano

serves 4

This Italian-American-style recipe breaks the cardinal (Italian) rule that you never, ever put cheese with fish, lest you overwhelm its delicate flavor. But here, a toasty, lightly cheesy bread crumb mixture makes a perfect coating for haddock, a thick, flaky white fish that is still affordable and plentiful in eastern waters. Any similarly textured fish, such as flounder or cod, can be substituted.

1 pound skinless haddock or other mild, flaky white fish, cut into 4 pieces

Coarse salt and freshly ground black pepper

1 teaspoon extra-virgin olive oil, plus more for drizzling and coating the pan

2 tablespoons Dijon mustard

½ cup panko bread crumbs or coarse bread crumbs (preferably dry, but fresh will work, too)

¼ cup chopped fresh parsley leaves

2 tablespoons grated Parmesan cheese

1 garlic clove, minced

Finely grated zest of 1 lemon

1 lemon, halved (juice one half and cut the other half into 4 pieces, for serving)

2 teaspoons unsalted butter

1 Preheat the oven to 425°F. Season the fish on both sides with salt and pepper, and place on an oiled or parchment paper–lined baking pan. Whisk together the oil and mustard and spread the mixture over the top of the fish.

2 Combine the bread crumbs, parsley, cheese, garlic, lemon zest, and a drizzle of oil (enough to slightly moisten the mixture) in a bowl. Pile the bread crumb mixture on each piece of fish and gently press it down. Drizzle a scant ½ teaspoon lemon juice over each one. Dot the tops with butter. Bake until cooked through and golden brown on top, about 8 minutes, depending on the thickness of the fish. The fish should feel slightly firm when pressed with your finger. Serve each portion with a lemon wedge.

FREEZE THIS DISH FOR FAST, FRESH FISH

Should you find yourself with a large amount of fish—either a gift from a fishing friend or because there is a great deal that day at the fish counter—make up this recipe and freeze the extra for the future. Wrap uncooked individual portions in tightly sealed foil packets. Label, date, and freeze them for up to 8 weeks. When you remove the packets—one at a time or more—unwrap and put them straight into a preheated oven. Add 1 extra minute to the cooking time. The fish will be just as delicious after its stint in the freezer as it was the day you bought it.

fish fillet in parchment paper

serves 2

In my house of dishwashing rebels, I'll do anything I can to promote a quick-and-easy cleanup. One mess-free way to cook fish fillets is to wrap them in parchment paper or, as it's called in France, *en papillote*. Once heated, steam builds inside the parchment package, creating a moist environment and causing the package to puff up dramatically. Cooking fish like this is an excellent way to impart flavor with minimal, if any, fat. Out of the oven, there's a *"ta da"* moment, too, when everyone cuts open their package (be careful, though—the steam is hot!).

2 bass, small snapper, or other mild, semifirm skinless white fish fillets

1 roasted red bell pepper, peeled, seeded, and cut into strips (see page 65), or jarred

2 teaspoons unsalted butter, softened

1 teaspoon capers, chopped

1 teaspoon finely grated lemon zest

4 fresh basil leaves, thinly sliced

Lemon wedges, for serving

2 cups cooked rice, or ½ baguette, torn, for serving

1. Preheat the oven to 400°F. Cut parchment paper into two 14-inch-long pieces. Lay 1 fish fillet on each one. Lay the peppers over each fillet.

2. Mash together the butter, capers, and lemon zest. Divide and place a dollop on top of each piece of fish. Scatter the basil over the fish.

3. Fold the parchment paper over the fish. Crimp the edges to make two half-moons and place on a baking sheet. Bake in the oven for 8 minutes.

4. Serve each package on a plate. Tear open and serve with lemon wedges and a scoop of rice or piece of torn baguette inside.

ABOUT PARCHMENT PAPER

I can't say enough about the many uses for nonstick and heat-resistant parchment paper.

- Place a piece on a wooden cutting board when working with raw fish, chicken, or meat.

- Use instead of butter or a silicone pad to line a baking sheet.

- Wrap up hunks of cheese and tape closed (it'll "breathe" and stay fresh longer).

- Place under dough when rolling it out, which makes it easy to move the dough in and out of the refrigerator if it becomes too warm to work with.

- Roll into a cone, snip off the tip, and use in place of a piping bag for icings or pastry fillings.

tangy grilled and glazed salmon

serves 4

One strong presence meets another in this dish, and the results are sublime. The tangy vinegar-basil sauce beautifully balances the rich flavor of the grilled salmon—even those who are hesitant when it comes to fish will love this. Serve it with the Ginger Rice (page 139). *Photo on page 94.*

1 cup balsamic vinegar

Finely grated zest and juice of 1 lemon, lime, or small orange

1 large basil sprig (about 1 cup leaves)

Vegetable oil

1 pound skin-on salmon, cut into 4 pieces

1 Combine the vinegar, citrus zest and juice, and basil in a small saucepan. Simmer until reduced by half and thickened to a glaze, about 8 minutes.

2 Meanwhile, prepare the grill or preheat a grill pan. Oil the skin of the salmon and place it on the grill, skin side down. Brush some glaze over the top of each piece, cover the grill, and cook through, 3 to 4 minutes, glazing a few more times during cooking.

spicy shrimp tacos

serves 4 to 6

Plump shrimp are tossed with a fresh combination of spicy green chilies, herbaceous cilantro, and tangy lime juice, folded into warm corn tortillas, and topped with juicy tomatoes and crisp lettuce. These ingredients, so favored in Mexican cooking, deliver big, assertive flavors that need no cheese or cream to satisfy that south-of-the-border hankering. I like to combine oil and butter for sautéing the shrimp (and many other things, truth be told)—the oil withstands the high heat while the butter brings flavor.

1 pound medium-large shrimp, peeled

Coarse salt and ground red pepper, such as cayenne, or black pepper

1 tablespoon extra-virgin olive oil

1 tablespoon unsalted butter

1 large fresh green chili, such as serrano or jalapeño

6 garlic cloves, minced

Juice of 1 lime

1½ cups minced fresh cilantro leaves

12 corn tortillas, toasted and stacked in a towel to steam

3 tomatoes, cored and chopped

½ head romaine lettuce, shredded

1 lime, cut into 12 wedges, for serving

1 Pat the shrimp dry with a towel and season all over with salt and pepper. Heat a large skillet over medium-high heat. Swirl in the oil. When it shimmers, add the butter and let it melt. Add the shrimp in a single layer and cook, without moving, for 2 minutes. Flip the shrimp and add the chili and garlic. Stir continuously for 2 minutes more, regulating the heat to avoid burning the garlic.

2 Turn off the heat and stir in the lime juice and cilantro. Place a few shrimp in each tortilla, add some tomato and lettuce, and serve with lime wedges.

FROZEN SHRIMP

Keep a bag of shrimp in the freezer. It's a great convenience item that thaws quickly, and you can pull out as many or as few pieces as you need at one time.

You can either transfer the shrimp to the refrigerator in the morning and they'll be defrosted by dinnertime, or place the bag in a bowl under a cool trickle of water for 20 minutes. (In fact, much of the "fresh" shrimp in the seafood case is thawed by the store; most shrimp are flash-frozen on boats immediately after being caught.) Look for ones harvested in the United States (which I prefer to those farmed from Asia) and use them for these speedy dinners.

Simple soup: heat some broth, add chopped vegetables, and drop the shrimp directly into the pot; simmer until pink and cooked through.

Fast pasta sauce: thaw shrimp and sauté them in olive oil with garlic, crushed red pepper flakes, and lemon zest. Add some white wine and lemon juice, and serve with pasta or crusty bread.

Quick fried rice: sauté minced garlic, ginger, and scallion in very hot vegetable oil. After a minute, add thawed, frozen shrimp and stir continuously until they are cooked through and pink. Stir in some cold leftover rice and a couple of tablespoons of fish sauce or soy sauce.

shrimp curry

serves 4 to 6

When our son (and professional chef) Miles returned from a tour of Thailand, he made this dish frequently. It's a typical Thai-style curry, which is easy to throw together if you keep a jar of store-bought curry paste on hand (see opposite). And it cooks in under 30 minutes! Miles regards this recipe as a basic guideline; he'll make it with pretty much any available vegetable in the fridge, and often swaps out shrimp for shredded chicken or pork. Or he makes it entirely vegetarian. Serve it with rice or rice noodles.

2 tablespoons vegetable oil

3 celery stalks, thinly sliced

2 bell peppers, red and/or green, cored, seeded, and sliced

3 Thai bird chilies or other small hot chilies, seeded (if concerned about heat) and minced

4 garlic cloves, minced

1 shallot, minced

2 inches of fresh ginger, peeled and grated

Coarse salt

3 tablespoons red curry paste

Two 14-ounce cans coconut milk

2 tablespoons fish sauce

1 pound shrimp, peeled

Freshly ground black pepper

Crushed red pepper flakes

1 head broccoli, cut into florets

4 cups cooked rice, or 8 ounces rice noodles, cooked, for serving

1 cup roughly chopped fresh cilantro leaves, for serving

1 lime, cut into wedges, for serving

1 Heat a shallow braising pan over medium-high heat and swirl in 1 tablespoon of the oil. Stir in the celery, bell peppers, chilies, garlic, shallot, ginger, and a pinch of salt and cook, stirring continuously until softened, 1 to 2 minutes.

2 Lower the heat to medium and stir in the curry paste to combine with the vegetables. Cook for about 2 minutes. Pour in the coconut milk and fish sauce and let simmer, partially covered, for about 15 minutes.

3 Meanwhile, pat the shrimp dry with a towel, and season all over with salt, black pepper, and red pepper flakes. Heat a large sauté pan over high heat. Swirl in the remaining 1 tablespoon oil and add the shrimp in a single layer. Sear the shrimp on one side, without moving, until golden brown, about 1½ minutes.

4 Add the broccoli to the coconut curry mixture, then add the shrimp. Increase the heat to high, cover, and cook until the shrimp is opaque and the broccoli is tender, about 5 minutes. Serve the shrimp in bowls over rice or noodles, garnished with the chopped cilantro and lime wedges.

ABOUT CURRY PASTE

Unless you have the time and money to procure the right ingredients and grind your own chilies, onions, garlic, spices, and herbs, it's totally okay to use a store-bought curry paste. Generally available as either a red or green paste, a small jar will last in your refrigerator for several months. I like the offerings on TempleofThai.com, and lots of grocery stores carry the red and green variety from ThaiKitchen.com.

Use these sauces carefully until you become familiar with their various heats. Some are more fiery than others, and you'll have to try a few before you decide which ones your family likes. Keep a few different kinds—some are called "sauce" while others are labeled "paste"—in the fridge to use with various dishes.

SONG FOR SARDINES

Canned sardines need to be in your life if they are not already (for real, get past your preconceived notions about fish in tins!).

They are high in the important omega fatty acids, vitamin B12, vitamin D, and calcium, and super-high in protein (sardines consume microscopic plants called plankton, not prey items). Devoid of mercury, they're one hell of a convenient health food. And they're eco-friendly—sardines mature quickly and spawn several times a year, and so replenish their numbers. For goodness sake, what more do you want from a food? That it tastes good, right? Well, move over, tuna—sardines are the new superstar. This fish tastes good and is affordable and transportable—there is always a tin in my purse!

HOW TO EAT SARDINES

straight from the can (available in oil, water, or saucy options) ★ on a crispy rye cracker with a schmear of mustard ★ on a cracker with ground black pepper and a squeeze of lemon juice ★ on a baguette with sweet butter and sliced tomato ★ in place of tuna for a salad Niçoise ★ à la shrimp cocktail with a mixture of horseradish, ketchup, and lemon juice ★ smashed with capers, minced onions, fresh dill, olive oil, and vinegar for a sandwich filling ★ broken up and laid inside an avocado half with a dollop of Dijon mustard ★ combined with chopped boiled eggs and hot sauce and served on white toast

steamed lobster

serves 4

I've never understood boiling lobsters—leaving behind all that flavor in the water, which takes forever to bring to a boil, seems like a waste. Steaming in a large pot with a tight-fitting lid is the way to go in my book. The only real trick to making lobster is minimizing the inevitable mess. Over the years, we've amassed a collection of large platters, so each diner gets a platter, a lobster, and a ramekin of melted butter laced with lemon juice. We also put out plenty of paper napkins, claw crackers, kitchen shears, a big bowl for the detritus, and a large black garbage bag to tie the whole mess up in when we're done. Summer!

4 lobsters (I like 1½ pounders)

1 cup (2 sticks) unsalted butter, melted, for serving

2 lemons, cut into wedges, for serving

Pour 1 inch of water into a large pot and bring to a boil. Immediately add the lobsters, cover, and let steam for 15 minutes. The shells should all have transformed from blue to a uniform orange. Lift them from the pot with long-handled tongs and hold them over the sink or bowl to let any liquid drain before placing each lobster on a platter. Serve immediately with claw crackers, scissors, and little forks to lift out the meat. Divide the butter among 4 ramekins to serve, along with lemon wedges on the side.

basil-garlic bread

Sizzle a peeled garlic clove in some olive oil. Add some thinly sliced basil. Slice a baguette lengthwise, and brush with the garlic-herb oil. Broil until lightly golden. Cut into pieces and serve with the lobster.

steamed clams or mussels

serves 2 for dinner, 4 as a starter

Once you've procured fresh, cleaned clams or mussels, the hard part is over because this is one quick, easy, and delicious meal. Get the aromatics sautéing, add the mussels or clams, cover, and steam until they open—and that's pretty much it. Once the shells are open, the fabulous juice mixes with the other sautéed aromatics for a glorious broth. Make sure to serve some bread for dunking.

1 tablespoon extra-virgin olive oil, plus more for drizzling

¼ cup minced shallots, onions, or garlic

⅓ cup chopped soppressata, bacon, chorizo, or any other cured porky meat (about 2 ounces; optional)

1 large tomato, fresh or canned, chopped

1 fresh green or red chili or dried chili, minced (optional)

1 cup minced fresh herbs, such as cilantro, parsley, or mint, plus more for serving

2 dozen clams or mussels, scrubbed (and debearded, if using mussels; see below)

1 cup white or red wine, beer, stock, or water, or as needed

1 Heat a large pot with a tight-fitting lid over medium-high heat and swirl in the olive oil. When it shimmers, add the shallots and soppressata (if using) and sauté until translucent, 3 to 4 minutes. Stir in the tomato, chili, and fresh herbs. Cook for a couple of minutes to heat through.

2 Add the clams or mussels and pour in enough liquid to cover the bottom of the pan by ¼ inch. When the liquid is bubbling rapidly, cover and cook until the shellfish have just opened, 3 to 6 minutes, depending on their size and the number in the pan. Discard any that do not open. Scatter over more fresh herbs, drizzle with olive oil, and serve.

WORTH KNOWING

HOW TO CLEAN BIVALVES

No one likes sitting down to a delicious-looking (and smelling) bowl of mussels or clams and then chomping into a mouthful of sand. If the mussels are farmed, such as rope mussels (one of the few farmed seafoods I like), then a quick rinse with cold water and removal of the small "beards" are all that's necessary. Wild mussels need a little more elbow grease—scrub the shells with an abrasive brush or sponge and trim the beard, if necessary. Clams should be scrubbed all over, and their soaking water must be changed at least three times, until it appears clear. I add some cornmeal to the first batch of soaking water because the clams open up to consume it and subsequently purge any unwanted sea-floor dreck.

STRETCH YOUR STEAMED CLAMS

Steamed clams and their steaming broth are great to have on hand. Here's how to steam them. Once you have cleaned the clams (see opposite), put them in a large pot with a tight-fitting lid and add ¼ inch of water to the pot. Cover the pot and steam the clams until the shells open, about 6 minutes. Using a slotted spoon, remove the clams from the liquid and set aside. Strain that liquid through a cheesecloth-lined sieve. Now you have clam broth—the makings of several dishes.

Basic Chowder Roadmap

To start, sauté some chopped onions, potatoes, and bacon in a pot until soft. Pour in the strained clam broth, and an additional 8-ounce bottle of store-bought clam juice, fish stock (see tip on page 14), chicken stock, or water. Add the clams, a sprig of fresh thyme (or pinch of dried), and a little bit of milk or cream.

Basic Clam Pasta Sauce Roadmap

Pasta with clam sauce is a great favorite. Thinly slice some garlic and place it in a large bowl filled with ¾ cup extra-virgin olive oil. If you have time, let the garlic mixture sit for a couple of hours (or all day) to flavor the oil. Pour in the strained clam juice and cooked clams (either still in the shells or removed from the shells—or some of each). Toss the clams with cooked linguine, fresh chopped parsley, and crushed red pepper flakes.

Basic Seafood Salad Roadmap

To make a killer clam salad, remove the clam meat from the shells, chill, and toss it with Classic French Vinaigrette (page 201) and chopped fresh herbs. Serve over butter lettuce.

neo clams casino

serves 6 to 8 as an appetizer

Clams casino are in the lockbox of my taste memories—they were the special-occasion appetizer my family would order at restaurants in the '60s and '70s. Back then, the shells were overstuffed with too many garlic powder–infused bread crumbs—although that didn't stop me from scarfing them down. This update lets the clam flavor shine through with fewer crumbs and doubles the usual amounts of parsley and lemon zest for a much fresher taste.

2 dozen clams, preferably littlenecks

¼ cup bread crumbs

¼ cup chopped fresh parsley leaves

3 garlic cloves, minced

2 strips bacon or sliced pancetta, cooked and crumbled

Finely grated zest and juice of 1 lemon

½ teaspoon crushed red pepper flakes

Coarse salt

Extra-virgin olive oil

1 Place the clams in a large pot with a tight-fitting lid and add ¼ inch of water to the pot. Steam until the shells open, about 6 minutes. With a slotted spoon or ladle, lift the clams out of the pot, remove and discard one half of the shell on each clam, leaving the meat attached to the other (if the meat falls out during steaming, place it in an empty shell). Arrange the clams side by side in a baking dish.

2 Preheat the broiler and set the oven rack at least 4 inches from it. Combine the bread crumbs, parsley, garlic, bacon, lemon zest and juice, red pepper flakes, and a pinch of salt. Top each clam with a teaspoon of the bread crumb mixture and drizzle oil over the top. Broil until the mixture is bubbling and golden brown, about 3 minutes. Watch carefully as the bread crumbs will easily burn. Serve immediately.

PANTRY POWER

OPPOSITE: Fried Pasta Snack (page 123)

EQUIP YOUR KITCHEN

Grocery shopping can feel like a Sisyphean task: you go, you stock up—to such an extent that when you arrive home and get the bags inside, you truly think there is no earthly place for everything to fit in your kitchen—and then about five minutes after putting everything away, you open the refrigerator to find a gaping maw of nothingness. Or so it seems. Where did all that stuff go? (Oh, right, you ate it.)

But here's the thing: you don't have to succumb to take-out pizza just because your fridge is bare. You can turn to your pantry and freezer, those magical places where cans, cured meats, and packages live, where food can last for months or even years.

PANTRY

canned tomatoes • tomato paste • wine • chicken broth • dried beans • pasta • rice • egg noodles • olive oil • vinegar • anchovies • capers • potatoes • onions • shallots • garlic • pepper flakes • coconut milk

FRIDGE/FREEZER

lemons • limes • oranges • ginger • Parmesan • Pecorino Romano • butter • sausage • cabbage • raisins • currants • nuts • sesame seeds • Thai curry paste

PASTA PLAYBOOK

If you have some dry pasta in the cupboard, plus water, salt, a pot, and a flame, there's not much else you need to make a decent dinner.

My husband is a champion of the "rustle it up from nothing" school of cooking. Sometimes when I've stayed too late at work, I call one of my guys as I'm leaving and tell him to put a large pot of water on to boil (and chop some onions, find a random sausage, *anything*). Since I don't have to make the 15-minute stop at the grocery store, I can just come home and revel in the pantry's untold improv-cooking bounty. Olive oil, butter (or some yummy fat like bacon or duck left over from a previous recipe), tomato paste, garlic, vinegar, wine, herbs, bacon, chorizo, and a can of some liquid (chicken broth, perhaps) will get you to a meal. In even the loneliest crisper, I can usually scare up a carrot or piece of celery, maybe some fresh peppers, or even some cabbage.

I just build a little flavor base with the onion-garlic-shallot-bacon-sausage options, and then liquefy it (with broth, milk, or cream) to make a saucy coating for the noodles, while adding whatever bits of vegetables, pickles, meats, beans, or tinned fish I have on hand. (This is exactly what happened with the penne recipe on page 131.)

spaghetti and simple tomato sauce

serves 4

It would be a tight race if I had to equate one dish with happiness and comfort, but I think it would come down to this pasta—one I'd gladly eat every day. (If only it guaranteed to keep my weight optimal—ha!) There's nothing complicated or revolutionary about it. In fact, the recipe has been reduced to the simplest combination of ingredients and results in a formula that wraps me in solace every single time I eat it.

2 tablespoons olive oil

2 garlic cloves, minced

Pinch of crushed red pepper flakes (optional)

One 28-ounce can best-quality whole tomatoes, lightly pulsed in a blender or cut with a knife or scissors

½ teaspoon coarse salt

1 pound spaghetti (or any pasta)

Grated Parmesan cheese, for serving

1 Boil a large pot of water. Meanwhile, heat a saucepan over medium heat, swirl in the oil, and add the garlic and red pepper flakes (if using), stirring until the garlic lightly sizzles but does not brown, about 30 seconds.

2 Add the tomatoes and salt. Simmer over medium heat for at least 20 minutes and up to 30 minutes. Ten minutes before the sauce is ready, salt the boiling water and cook the spaghetti for 2 minutes shy of the package instructions and taste for doneness. Drain the pasta and toss with some sauce. For each serving, spoon on a little extra sauce and sprinkle with grated Parmesan cheese.

ABOUT CANNED TOMATOES

I've never met a canned tomato that I wouldn't at least *try*—from run-of-the-mill grocery versions to the fancy ones from specialty Italian markets like Eataly. Some are too sweet, some too tangy, some robust, and others bland—and price doesn't always determine the quality. Sample some options to see what you like—if one brand is too tangy, add a pinch of sugar. Too sweet? Add some salt. In recent years, my standby has been plain organic whole tomatoes from Muir Glen, for their balanced flavor and texture. They're ideal to use both when they are the main ingredient (as in this recipe), or when they are one among many, as in Beef-Stuffed Peppers and Squash (page 40). Stock your pantry with 28- and 14½-ounce cans whole tomatoes and use a blender to "chop" or puree, as necessary.

TWO MORE QUICK RED SAUCES FOR PASTA

Amatriciana: for this sauce, sauté a small minced red onion and two strips of chopped bacon in olive oil. Add a 28-ounce can of best-quality whole tomatoes, lightly pulsed in a blender or cut with a knife or scissors. Simmer for 30 minutes and then toss with a favorite cooked pasta.

Arrabbiata: to make this peppery sauce, sauté minced garlic and 2 small dried, crushed hot peppers, or 1 teaspoon crushed red pepper flakes. Add a 28-ounce can of best-quality whole tomatoes, lightly pulsed in a blender or cut with a knife or scissors. Simmer for 20 minutes. Combine with cooked pasta.

carbonara

serves 4 to 6

My sons loved this dish so much when they were little that it was the first dinner they learned to cook for themselves. Carbonara, as it's generally called, contains their holy trinity—bacon, eggs, and cheese—with the added bonus of that pantry star, pasta. All four of these ingredients lend themselves to variation, which is why there are so many different options for (and opinions about) carbonara—some use cream, some add parsley, some call for noodles other than spaghetti. Basic instructions follow here, with some extended options, in case you have the ingredients and want a few more layers of flavor.

3 large eggs

1 cup grated Parmesan cheese, plus more for serving

Freshly ground black pepper

8 ounces bacon or pancetta, sliced crosswise into ½-inch pieces

Coarse salt

2 garlic cloves, smashed and peeled (optional)

Splash of white wine (optional)

1 pound spaghetti (or any pasta noodle)

1 In a large serving bowl, whisk together the eggs, cheese, and pepper.

2 Cook the bacon in a large skillet over medium heat until just crispy, 8 to 10 minutes. If using garlic cloves, add them with the bacon and cook until lightly golden; remove them before serving. If desired, skim off some of the excess fat. Add the wine, if using, and let the mixture bubble away for a minute.

3 Meanwhile, boil a large pot of water. Generously salt the water, boil the pasta for 2 minutes shy of the package instructions, and taste for doneness—the pasta should be al dente. Drain. Add the hot noodles and bacon mixture directly to the bowl of eggs. Toss everything together quickly until the noodles are evenly coated (it's important to work quickly so the eggs cook gently and become a rich sauce without curdling). Make sure the bacon is evenly distributed throughout the pasta. Serve immediately topped with Parmesan.

SUBSTITUTING SALTY PORK PRODUCTS

I'm sure some people think what I am about to say is sacrilege, but here goes: if you don't have bacon, use pancetta or Spanish or cured chorizo. Essentially, their role is to impart a salty, porky underlayer of flavor to a sauce or stew. So if a recipe calls for pancetta and you only have bacon in your fridge, don't be afraid to use it. It will do the job just fine.

fried pasta snack

serves 4 to 6

Imagine a dish that maximizes the covetable crunch that lasagna noodles get around the bubbly hot edges. This is it. The pasta, tangled together with a little sauce, crisps to a golden crunch on the outside and stays soft in the middle. Every time I make it for a friend, they have one of those lightbulb moments, as they realize, "I have to make this at home!" And every time I make it for my sons, there isn't a shred of spaghetti left. I make this with leftover pasta, but you can cook spaghetti fresh to make it anytime.

8 ounces cooked spaghetti

⅓ cup prepared tomato sauce

1 tablespoon extra-virgin olive oil

Grated Parmesan cheese

Toss the pasta with the tomato sauce to coat completely. Heat a 12-inch cast-iron skillet over medium-low heat and swirl in the oil. Spread the pasta in the pan in one layer. Cook, without moving it, until the bottom is crisp and golden brown, 10 to 15 minutes. Invert the pan to turn the pasta upside down onto a plate, the golden side facing up. Top with grated Parmesan and cut into wedges.

pinky pasta

serves 4 to 6

Sometimes a depleted pantry—like the one at my mother's house—can throw down a challenge. I remember arriving at her house to find not a single can of tomatoes on the shelves. (And this woman married an Italian?!) That evening, pinky pasta was born—created by using a little tomato paste—and has since been welcomed into our recipe routine, sometimes as the main course, and also as a side for meat and vegetables.

Coarse salt

8 ounces campanelle pasta (or other short macaroni)

2 tablespoons olive oil

1 to 2 garlic cloves, minced

3 tablespoons tomato paste

¾ cup chicken broth

Freshly ground black pepper

1 tablespoon unsalted butter

1 Boil a large pot of water. Generously salt the water and boil the pasta for 2 minutes shy of the package instructions. Taste for doneness and drain—the pasta should be al dente (soft but still firm, never mushy).

2 Heat the oil and the garlic in a small, deep skillet over medium heat. Cook, stirring, for 30 seconds, then add the tomato paste. Continue to cook, stirring, for 2 minutes. Pour in the broth and bring to a simmer. Simmer until slightly thickened, 3 to 5 minutes, and stir in the butter. Toss the pasta in the sauce to coat. Serve warm.

LIVESAVER LESSON

USE YOUR NOODLES

In traditional Italian cooking, there's a logic to pairing sauces with pastas. For instance, silken, creamy sauces are paired with long strands of pasta, while chunky, robust sauces cry out for short tubular or stumpy shapes so that the ingredients have a place to cling. While these are ideas to aspire to, home cooks don't have to subscribe to them. If your recipe calls for one type of noodle, it's not a federal offense to use another. Use what you have!

spaghetti with garlic three ways

serves 4

Garlic is such an amazing ingredient. It can be raw—rough and rugged—sautéed to a nutty brown, or baked to a soft, buttery sweetness. This recipe combines these three techniques into one dish with subtly layered flavors. When shopping for garlic, choose carefully: make sure the head has firm, snug-fitting cloves, smooth skin, and a heaviness for its size, like a large marble.

Coarse salt

1 pound spaghetti

½ cup extra-virgin olive oil

6 garlic cloves (2 thinly sliced, 2 minced, 2 smashed and peeled)

½ cup pasta water or chicken broth

1 cup grated Pecorino Romano cheese, plus more for serving

½ teaspoon freshly ground black pepper

1 Boil a large pot of water. Generously salt the water, and boil the pasta for 2 minutes shy of the package instructions. Taste for doneness and drain, reserving ½ cup of the pasta cooking water.

2 Meanwhile, heat the oil in a large skillet over medium-high heat. Add the sliced garlic and cook until golden brown, about 2 minutes, and remove from the skillet. Add the minced garlic and cook until fragrant but not colored, about 30 seconds.

3 Add the spaghetti and reserved pasta water or stock to the skillet and bring to a simmer. Remove from the heat and toss in the cheese, pepper, browned sliced garlic, and smashed garlic (leave the raw garlic cloves behind in the pan). Serve with additional grated cheese.

ABOUT PASTA WATER

Tap water is as good as free—there's no reason to be stingy with it when making pasta. Use plenty of water to boil your pasta, as much as you can. Fill a 5-quart pot three-quarters full. Granted, it'll take the water longer to boil, but what else were you planning on doing during those extra 2 or 3 minutes? The noodles will cook evenly if not crowded together in a small pot of water. Salt the boiling water generously (a couple teaspoons at least) just before dropping the pasta in. The salt adds needed flavor.

Post-boiling, save a cup or two of the pasta water: the cloudiness means it's swirling with residual starch, which will help to lightly thicken any type of sauce or topping. Mixed with a good amount of grated cheese, the water forms a creamy sauce; a couple of glugs of the pasta water will blend with the juices of any vegetables and marry them to the pasta.

fettuccine with lemon, herbs, and parmesan

serves 4

Lemon is often the amazing, elusive ingredient X, bringing a bright, tangy layer to so many pasta dishes. In this recipe, the yellow citrus is very much in the spotlight. The grated cheese, lemon juice, and starchy pasta water come together to create a delicate sauce that cloaks the noodles. Toss in some fresh peas or baby arugula for a more complete, one-dish meal.

Coarse salt

1 pound dried fettuccine or other long noodles, such as spaghetti

3 ounces Parmesan cheese, grated (about 1 cup), plus more for serving

Finely grated zest and juice of 1 lemon (about 2 tablespoons juice)

½ cup torn fresh mint, basil, or parsley leaves

1 tablespoon unsalted butter

1 tablespoon extra-virgin olive oil

Crushed red pepper flakes (optional)

1 Boil a large pot of water. Generously salt the water and boil the pasta for 2 minutes shy of the package instructions. Test for doneness and drain, reserving 1 cup of the pasta cooking water.

2 Transfer the pasta to a large warm bowl and mix in the reserved cooking water, cheese, lemon zest and juice, mint, butter, oil, and red pepper flakes, if you like. Divide among dishes, garnish with cheese, and serve immediately.

ABOUT LEMON ZEST

If your recipe calls for lemon juice, try adding a pinch of grated zest, too. It's richer and oilier and can be used in so many clever ways to enhance flavor. Use a Microplane grater or the side of a box grater to zest your lemon (or any citrus), taking care to avoid the bitter white pith. Use a potato peeler or sharp paring knife to peel off strips of zest.

Here are some other ideas for making good use of the zest (sometimes called the rind or peel):

- Mash some grated lemon zest into cream cheese and use in a cream cheese and smoked salmon sandwich.

- Mix the zest with ground black pepper for a salt-free seasoning.

- Boil some zest in equal parts sugar and water. Cool and use the infused syrup in lemonade or as a cocktail mixture with sparkling soda.

- Drop several large pieces of zest in a bottle and add vodka. Cork or screw on the top and let it infuse for a couple of weeks.

- Dry grated zest in a low oven until the moisture has evaporated. Grind in a blender with sugar. Dust over fresh fruit, pancakes, or French toast.

macaroni with sausage and kale

serves 4 to 6

Sausage and kale are perfect partners: the sausage is sweet and fatty, which counterbalances the kale's bitterness. Sausage meat has built-in seasonings, too, which imbue the sauce with richness and flavor without having to add a lot of extra ingredients.

Coarse salt

1 pound penne or other tubular pasta, such as ziti or fusilli

Extra-virgin olive oil

1 pound sweet Italian sausage

2 garlic cloves, minced

¼ teaspoon crushed red pepper flakes, plus more for serving

1 head lacinato kale or common kale, trimmed and thinly sliced

¾ cup grated Parmesan cheese, plus more for serving

1. Boil a large pot of water. Generously salt the water and cook the pasta for 2 minutes shy of the package instructions. Test for doneness and drain, reserving 2 cups of the pasta cooking water.

2. Meanwhile, heat a large sauté pan over high heat. Swirl in the olive oil. When it shimmers, squeeze the sausage meat from their casings into the pan. Sauté until the meat begins to brown, about 4 minutes. Stir in the garlic and red pepper flakes. Add the kale and stir to combine. Cook until the kale is tender, 6 to 8 minutes.

3. Add the pasta, cheese, and the reserved cooking water to the sausage mixture and stir to combine. Divide among bowls and top with more grated cheese, a drizzle of olive oil, and a sprinkle of red pepper flakes.

ITALIAN CHEESE: THE TWO Ps

Here are a few words on the most commonly used grating cheeses.

Let me offer you a primer on Parmesan cheese. First and foremost: buy it in wedges, not in cans. Invest in the good stuff, like Parmigiano-Reggiano, the hard cow's-milk cheese that is the most elite in terms of flavor and style, and is only made in certain areas as designated by Italian law. It's priced to match its pedigree, which is why I buy it in chunks to get my money's worth out of every shred. I keep it properly wrapped in the refrigerator (completely covered in parchment paper or plastic wrap), and use it for nibbling whole as well as for grating. There is nothing wrong with Grana Padano, a Parmesan-type cheese that's less expensive and delivers a similarly satisfying, salty-savory flavor as Parmigiano-Reggiano.

Pecorino Romano is saltier, sharper, and less subtle than Parmesan, but also less expensive. It lends a good depth of flavor to meatballs. One of my Italian grandmothers used it exclusively, and my mom mixed it with Parmesan for the best of both worlds. Sometimes, it's a waste to use the expensive aged Parmesan in cooking (like when a whole cup is needed in meatball meat).

If you buy and use large chunks of grating cheese, keep the hollowed-out rinds in the freezer and add them to a soup pot for extra flavor. If you forget about a wedge and find it months later in the bottom of your refrigerator, wearing a fuzzy green coat, just cut the mold away—the cheese will be fine.

penne with cabbage, bacon, and currants

serves 6 to 8

Cabbage is the canned good of the vegetable world. A head of cabbage will not only outlast almost any other perishable in your fridge, but it is incredibly affordable and offers abundant volume. Depending on how it's cooked or cut, it can yield all kinds of different flavors, from crisp and peppery in coleslaw to beautifully caramelized, as in this dish.

Coarse salt

1 pound penne pasta

1 tablespoon extra-virgin olive oil

1 small red onion, sliced

2 garlic cloves, minced

2 strips bacon

¼ teaspoon crushed red pepper flakes

½ head red or green cabbage, finely shredded

¼ cup currants

Grated zest of ½ lemon, plus ½ lemon

3 tablespoons red wine vinegar

½ cup milk

½ cup grated Parmesan cheese, plus more for serving

1 Boil a large pot of water. Generously salt the water and cook the pasta for 2 minutes shy of the package instructions. Test for doneness and drain, reserving 1 cup of the pasta cooking water.

2 Meanwhile, heat a large sauté pan over high heat. Swirl in the oil. When it shimmers, add the onions, garlic, bacon, and red pepper flakes and sauté until the onions soften and the bacon fat is slightly rendered, 2 to 3 minutes. Add the cabbage, currants, and lemon zest and cook until the cabbage is slightly caramelized and barely tender, about 6 minutes.

3 Add the vinegar, stirring to deglaze the pan. Add the reserved pasta water, milk, and cheese, stirring to melt the cheese. Add the penne to the pan. Remove from the heat, squeeze the lemon half over the pasta, and toss to combine. Serve immediately with extra cheese.

BETTING ON BEANS AND LOVING LEGUMES

Please, people: I *implore* you to make friends with beans. Black beans, red beans, pinto beans, kidney beans, navy beans, and chickpeas are all nutrient-dense powerhouses and flavor caravans. No greater value for your dollar and mealtime health exists. Canned beans are a handy, delicious, and affordable protein, available in virtually any variety you want. There are lots of good options out there (look for the low-sodium and organic varieties). Some brands can be a little mushy for my taste but perhaps not for yours; experiment until you find a preferred type.

Slightly more time-consuming (though mostly hands-off) and even more affordable (i.e., downright cheap) are dried beans. Buy them in the bulk bins at a good grocery store or natural foods store and soak and cook them yourself. You can do this on the stovetop, in the slow cooker, or in a pressure cooker. With a big batch in hand, you have the elemental ingredient for many filling, affordable, and family-friendly meals. Cook the soaked beans (see page 138 for instructions) while you're puttering around the house, doing laundry, or taking care of other chores. Use the beans right away or cool and freeze them in pint containers. Pulling a small container from the freezer becomes as convenient as opening a can.

Lentils are perhaps one of the best introductions to legumes. They are small and meaty and cook in less than 20 minutes from start to finish. We eat lentil soup weekly because there are always some lentils in the pantry, a scrap of carrot and celery in the crisper, and an onion in the cupboard. (Yes, even cooking experts have food-shopping challenges!) Homemade lentil soup tastes far from a scraped-together meal, especially if topped with big crunchy croutons (recipe in *Mad Hungry: Feeding Men & Boys*). Once cooked, lentils are ready to be dressed for a Lentil Salad (page 200) or cooked into one of my all-time favorite dishes, mujadara (page 134), a one-pot combination of rice and lentils that is widely eaten throughout the Middle East.

Whether canned or dried, there's no better way to cook on a budget than to incorporate legumes into your diet. Black Beans and Rice (page 138) has been an essential part of our regular diet for years. It feeds large groups, and whatever condiments you can top the beans with further enliven this hearty and satisfying meal. These might be chopped tomatoes, avocados, onions, cilantro, or grated cheese. If you're a meat lover, a tiny amount of bacon, chorizo, or other porky product can flavor your bean pot, too. Make a vegetarian version by first sautéing vegetables (like diced fresh peppers, onions, carrots, tomatoes, and garlic) in oil for about 10 minutes, softening them to meld into a concentrated seasoning paste before adding the beans. We made the decision when the kids were little to serve beans in our home every week, a routine that has continued even now that they are grown. If you are new to cooking, commit yourself to learning to love this great food source.

ceci di pasta

If you are a rookie bean eater, start with chickpeas, which have a firm texture and mild flavor that blends well with other ingredients. They let you go meatless without missing anything, especially when mixed with pasta like my Italian great-aunt used to do for (pre–Vatican II) meatless Friday dinners. Here's how: start with small cooked pasta shells and mix them in a simple sauce of sautéed olive oil, minced garlic, puréed tomatoes, chicken broth, and chickpeas, topped with grated Parmesan cheese.

my mujadara

serves 6 to 8

This recipe is based loosely on mujadara, a staple of the Middle East that has many variations depending on the country or even the community. It's often served as a side dish, but I like it as a main course, especially when serving a group. If you have time, pan-fried caramelized onion slices are a great garnish (see page 178).

2 cups lentils

2 tablespoons extra-virgin olive oil

1 onion, thinly sliced

6 garlic cloves, minced

1 tablespoon ground cumin

1 teaspoon ground cinnamon

½ teaspoon ground turmeric

¼ teaspoon cayenne pepper

2 cups white basmati or jasmine rice

3 cups water

2 teaspoons coarse salt

1. Place the lentils in a medium pot and add water to cover by 1 inch. Boil until just tender, about 15 minutes, depending on the size and age of the lentils. Drain.

2. Meanwhile, heat a medium pot over high heat and swirl in the oil. When it shimmers, add the onions and garlic and cook until lightly caramelized, about 10 minutes. Regulate the heat to avoid burning the garlic. Stir in the cumin, cinnamon, turmeric, and cayenne and cook for 2 minutes. Add the rice and stir to lightly toast and coat with spices, about 3 minutes. Stir the cooked lentils into the rice.

3. Pour in the water and add the salt. Bring to a rolling boil over high heat, reduce the heat to low and simmer, covered, until the liquid has been absorbed, about 20 minutes.

WORTH KNOWING

HOW TO KEEP SPICES FRESH

It's not a legit spice rack without an odd little bottle of an outlier ingredient that you use exactly 1.8 times a year. (They can't all be cumin!) For any spices that you use less than once a week, keep them fresh by stowing them, still in their jars or decanted into a zip-top plastic bag, in a large plastic container with a lock-on lid. Store the container in a cool, dry place, away from light. And when you do need that random, long-neglected spice, sniff it first to assure that it still retains some power.

RICE WHISPERER

One day, when I was teaching a friend to cook, I pulled out a bag of Arborio rice and proceeded to cook it as I would white rice. My friend was utterly dumbfounded to discover you could do something other than make risotto with this Italian rice. "You mean it's just effin' rice?" she hooted. This cracked me up—and clued me in to how easy it is to get confused by this elemental grain. But I encourage you to get comfortable with rice: don't be intimidated by all the varieties available today.

Plain Cooked Rice

Most package instructions suggest 1 cup rice to 2 cups liquid, but that can lead to some pretty mushy stuff. I prefer one part rice to one and a half parts liquid (be it water, broth, or a mixture), and a large pinch of salt. Bring the rice and liquid to a boil, cover, and reduce the heat to low. Cook for 20 minutes; 40 minutes for brown rice. If a friend cooks her rice a different way, it doesn't mean you're doing it wrong. If it works, it works. Don't question it. There are as many rice-cooking techniques in the world as there are cultures.

Rice cookers are invaluable if you eat a lot of rice. Or designate one pot a rice pot—one with which to practice rice perfection. A two-quart heavy-bottomed pot with a snug lid is a good place to start.

Also, if you're in for a penny, you might as well be in for a pound: double your desired amount every time you make rice and store it in zip-top plastic bags stacked flat in the freezer. Defrost in the fridge or place a bag in hot water for about 5 minutes, weighted to keep it submerged. There is no greater friend to leftovers (or last-minute meal prep) than rice. Put an egg on it, stir-fry it with vegetables or meat, or make it into rice pudding.

OTHER PREFERRED PREPARATIONS

Brazilian Rice
A Brazilian friend of mine is mystified by our slavish attention to package instructions and kitchen timers. She learned from her mom the "thumb technique": dump the desired amount of rice in the pot and cover with water to the depth of your thumb to its knuckle. Her method produced one of the most delicious rice dishes I've eaten:

Mince a clove of garlic and then mash it with a teaspoon of salt. Sizzle it in oil long enough to release its fragrance but not so long that it turns golden or burns. Add the rice. Pour water over the rice until top of rice is covered by 1 inch. Bring to a rapid rolling boil, cover, reduce the heat to a simmer, and cook for 15 minutes. Remove from the heat and let rest, covered, for 5 minutes.

Mexican Rice
Today I make two different Mexican rice dishes somewhat similar to the hamburger, rice, and canned tomatoes meal my mom used to make. I learned authentic techniques in Mexico and have never looked back. One is red and the other green, starting with cooking the rice with onions in oil before adding either puréed tomatoes (for red rice) or puréed cilantro and fresh green chili (for green rice). In both versions chicken stock is the liquid. Sometimes, frozen or fresh corn kernels or peas are added to the top of the rice before covering the pan to cook. Scoop a large spoonful of refried beans over that rice, and I am one happy camper.

Asian Rice
The variety of rice styles used in Asian cooking vary from plain steamed white rice to Japanese sushi rice seasoned with vinegar (a high art in itself), Thai-style sticky rice, Hainanese chicken rice, Chinese congee porridge (made from rice), and many other regional types and styles. When I cook spicy Asian main dishes at home, I accompany them with basic unseasoned white rice. If the main dish is only mildly Asian-flavored, I serve a seasoned rice such as Ginger Rice or Coconut Rice (page 139), an entirely personal shortcut to achieve restaurant-style satisfaction.

black beans and rice

serves 4

This is the simple, affordable meal that sustained our young family when the grocery budget was slim. Today, it's as loved as many other, much more expensive options. That's what happens when a recipe is used to nourish more than just the body. It becomes a part of that memory bank, the stuff that cravings are made of.

3 tablespoons olive oil

1 medium white onion, chopped

2 garlic cloves, minced

¾ teaspoon coarse salt

½ teaspoon ground cumin

¼ teaspoon freshly ground black pepper

¼ teaspoon dried oregano

Two 15½-ounce cans black beans, drained, or 30 ounces cooked dry beans (see below)

½ cup water

3 cups cooked white or brown rice (page 136)

1 avocado, pitted, peeled, and chopped (optional, for serving)

1 lime, cut into wedges, for serving

1 Heat 2 tablespoons of the oil in a large sauté pan over medium-high heat. When it shimmers, add half the onion, garlic, and salt and cook, stirring occasionally, until the onion is soft and translucent, about 3 minutes.

2 Stir in the cumin, pepper, and oregano and cook for 1 minute more. Add the beans and water and continue cooking, stirring occasionally, until the beans are warmed through, about 5 minutes. Remove from the heat and stir in the remaining 1 tablespoon oil.

3 Serve the black beans over rice, garnished with the remaining onion, the avocado (if using), and lime wedges.

WORTH KNOWING

HOW TO COOK DRIED BEANS

To use dried beans, soak them in water to cover overnight or for at least 6 hours. Or you can "quick soak" beans: place them in a large pot, cover with water, and bring to a boil, then remove from the heat and let sit for about 1 hour. Now they are ready to cook. To do so, drain the water, add new water, and simmer until the beans are tender, 1 to 2 hours. Use these beans as directed in step 2 for Black Beans and Rice.

ginger rice

makes 1½ quarts; serves 4 to 6

We eat a lot of rice in our household. It's the perfect base or side dish for so many recipes, and can stretch just about any meal to serve more folks. Sometimes it's nice to alter your basic cooking style a bit, especially with this sort of staple. I like to serve this with Asian Pantry Marinated Steak (page 32).

2 teaspoons safflower oil	**1** Heat a saucepan over medium-high heat. Swirl in the oil. When it shimmers, add the onion and ginger. Sauté, stirring continuously, for 1 minute. Add the sesame seeds and rice and cook until the rice begins to toast to a light golden color.
¼ onion or 1 shallot, finely minced	
One 2-inch piece of fresh ginger, peeled and minced	
1 tablespoon sesame seeds	
1½ cups rice	**2** Add the water and the salt, stir briefly just to distribute the rice evenly, and bring the water to a rolling boil over high heat. Reduce the heat to low and simmer, covered, until the liquid has been absorbed, about 20 minutes.
3 cups water	
½ teaspoon coarse salt	

coconut rice

makes 2 quarts; serves 6

For a vegetarian meal, this white rice variation is delicious with Indian-Spiced Cauliflower and Carrots (page 151). It also works beautifully any time sweet, mellow coconut flavors are desired to complement a meat dish, such as the Spicy-Sweet Ginger Pork Chops (page 13).

2 cups basmati or jasmine rice, rinsed	Place the rice, coconut milk, salt, and water in a pan. Bring to a boil. Cover, reduce the heat to low, and cook until the liquid has been absorbed, about 20 minutes. Fluff the rice with a fork and stir in the scallions.
One 13½-ounce can light coconut milk	
1 teaspoon coarse salt	
1¼ cups water	
1 scallion, thinly sliced	

easy arborio rice

serves 6

Don't assume Arborio rice is only for risotto. Rather than letting it sit in your cupboard forever after one risotto attempt, prepare it as you would any rice. It produces a squat, meaty kernel, delicious served with Cacciatore (page 59) or Haddock Italiano (page 102).

2 tablespoons olive oil

1 small yellow onion, chopped (about 1 cup)

1 teaspoon coarse salt

2 cups Arborio rice

2 garlic cloves, minced

2 cups chicken broth

1 cup water

1 Heat the oil in a 3- to 4-quart saucepan over medium-high heat. When it shimmers, add the onions and salt and sauté until the onions are translucent, about 3 minutes. Add the rice and garlic to the pan and sauté until the rice is toasted and fragrant, about 2 minutes.

2 Add the broth and water to the pan. Bring to a boil, stir once, cover, and reduce the heat to low. Simmer the rice, covered, until the liquid has been absorbed, 18 to 20 minutes. Remove the pan from the heat and let stand, covered, for 5 minutes before serving.

ABOUT RICE

In America, **basmati** and **jasmine rice** have become as ubiquitous and popular as standard-issue white, long-grain American rice. They are often called for interchangeably in recipes, yet their origins are different. Jasmine is originally from Thailand, while basmati is from the foothills of the Himalayas in northern India and Pakistan. Many rice growers in the United States are now selling home-grown varieties of both, such as Texmati, which is literally just jasmine rice varieties cultivated in Texas. Its kernels are longer and thinner than short-grain American rice, resulting in a dry, fluffy texture. I tend to use either jasmine or basmati rice when I'm cooking anything from the Asian or Middle Eastern diaspora, as both varieties have a complementary fragrant, almost floral, flavor.

The kernels of **Arborio, Carnaroli, Valencia, Bomba,** and **short-grain sushi rice** are generally less than twice as long as they are wide. They are all chewier and stickier than their long-grain cousins.

nesting noodle rice pilaf

serves 8 to 10

Sometimes a happy accident—i.e., a near-empty fridge but a well-stocked pantry—gives birth to a new and beloved dish. This is one of them. It's a riff on a pilaf, which often marries rice and noodles in a single dish. Here, I use little noodle nests, which are formed from dry pasta and sold in large packages. It serves a crowd and would be good with any saucy dish.

4 tablespoons (½ stick) unsalted butter

1½ pounds mushrooms, such as button or cremini, sliced

3 teaspoons coarse salt

4 shallots, minced (about ¼ cup)

5 cups Arborio rice

9 cups chicken broth

1 pound tagliatelle noodle nests

1 Heat a 14-inch skillet or cast-iron braiser over medium-high heat. Add 2 tablespoons of the butter and when it melts, sauté the mushrooms and 1 teaspoon of the salt until the mushrooms' liquid has evaporated and the mushrooms are nut-brown, 5 to 7 minutes. Add the shallots and 1 tablespoon of the butter during the last couple of minutes of cooking.

2 Add the remaining 1 tablespoon butter, remaining 2 teaspoons salt, and the rice. Stir to coat and lightly toast the rice for about 3 minutes.

3 Meanwhile, bring the broth to a boil in a separate pot. Make several indentations in the rice and nestle in the noodle nests. Fit in as many nests as space will allow. Pour the hot broth over the rice and pasta, reduce the heat to low, cover the pot, and cook until the rice is tender and the noodles are cooked through, about 25 minutes.

OPPOSITE: Fresh Tomato and Corn Mélange with Steamed Green Beans (page 158)

CHOP YOUR OWN BROCCOLI

Cooking is a life-affirming gesture—both of self-reliance (when we prepare meals for ourselves) and generosity (when we feed others). One thing that means a lot to me is chopping my own vegetables. Let me use broccoli to make a case for doing this yourself. Rather than buying the sealed bag of prechopped florets, buy a full head and cut it yourself. I promise you, doing so will only eat up about four extra minutes of your life. You can clean it and cut it the way you choose—and actually get to see it for the miracle that it is. (Broccoli is crazy cool! Each one of those tiny green buds at the top of the "tree" could become its own flower!)

The supermarket is filled with shortcut products designed for convenience—minced garlic, roasted chicken, garlic-herb-sundried-tomato hummus—but they mask your connection to food. All these items aim to save time, and are admissible in a pinch, so you can invest that time in something else. But what is a more valuable use of time than self-care? Or caring for loved ones? There is no better way to nurture friends, family, and ourselves than to consistently prepare meals. If you stick with cooking, you will not be disappointed. I bet you'll even end up loving it. Maybe a few things won't be as delicious as you'd hoped, but with time and practice, you can ensure that the desired flavors and textures will be achieved. Even your failures can provide many funny memories (once, in a cooking class with me as the so-called "expert," a doomed chocolate cake turned into hot fudge sauce, right before my students' eyes).

Practice the daily ritual of cooking, and it can act as ballast in rough waters. And I don't mean making fancy meals or hosting little dinner parties. I mean something as simple as establishing a daily rhythm via food: brew a pot of tea or coffee, squeeze some fresh juice, simmer some oatmeal, or even just butter some toast. Let these rituals ease you into the day. The key is in seeing that the making of food is as much of a pleasure as the eating of it. When home-cooked meals and moments are peppered throughout a busy life, peace and relaxation are possible. See cooking as an active meditation. To do so is to build a foundation for your life—a predictable place of solace. The kitchen can become your bunker—that safe and secure location.

broccoli two-step

serves 4

Broccoli is a vegetable that is absolutely delicious if cooked properly—and nothing short of nasty if cooked poorly. Never again serve drab, dull-green, mushy broccoli that fills the kitchen with an *icky* aroma! Cook it right and watch it become a family favorite.

1 head broccoli

1 tablespoon olive oil

2 garlic cloves, sliced

Pinch of crushed red pepper flakes

½ teaspoon coarse salt

1 Clean and separate the broccoli into small florets and then slice the florets lengthwise into smaller pieces. Submerge in water to clean. Peel the stalks and slice into thin coins.

2 Heat a large skillet over medium-high heat. Swirl in the oil. When it shimmers, add the garlic, a hefty pinch of red pepper flakes, and the drained broccoli pieces. Toss to coat with the oil and seasonings. Add ¼ cup water and the salt. Turn the broccoli over and over until the water has evaporated, about 3 minutes, and the broccoli is sizzling in the oil. Continue cooking until just tender, 2 to 3 minutes more.

ABOUT BROCCOLINI

Broccolini looks similar to broccoli but is actually a hybrid variety of broccoli and a Japanese vegetable called kai-lan. It has long, thin stalks and small, loose florets with the occasional yellow blossom mixed in. It's sweeter and slightly more tender than broccoli and can be cooked the same way—it's a great addition to a stir-fry (page 148).

broccoli francese

serves 4 to 6

I don't love the trick of hiding vegetables in treats, like cupcakes made with puréed spinach. I prefer to inculcate the veggie-averse (of all ages!) by spotlighting a vegetable's flavor alongside other delicious bedfellows. In this case, the cheesy eggs surround and infuse the green florets with a golden savor. Just about everyone will like the broccoli here—and then be emboldened to eat it another time sautéed in oil and garlic and then even (deep breath!) simply steamed.

1 head broccoli, separated into small florets, stem peeled and thinly sliced into coins

6 large eggs

¾ cup grated Parmesan or Romano cheese, plus more for serving

Coarse salt and freshly ground black pepper

2 teaspoons extra-virgin olive oil

1 lemon, cut into wedges, for serving

1 Bring ½ inch of water to a boil in a 3-quart saucepan. Add the broccoli, cover, and steam until crisp-tender, 3 to 4 minutes. Drain. In a bowl, whisk together the eggs, cheese, a pinch of salt, and a couple grinds of pepper.

2 Heat a medium nonstick or well-seasoned cast-iron skillet over high heat. Swirl in the oil. When it shimmers, scatter the cooked broccoli over the bottom of the skillet. Pour the egg mixture over the broccoli and swirl the skillet to cover the bottom of the pan. Cook until golden on the bottom, about 3 minutes. Flip and cook until the eggs are set, 3 to 4 minutes more. (It should flip easily, but if you prefer, place a plate slightly larger than the skillet on top of the pan and turn the "pancake" over onto it, cooked side up. Then slide it back into the pan.)

3 Slide the cooked eggs onto a cutting board and cut into bite size-pieces for snacking or appetizers, or into wedges to serve as a side dish. Sprinkle with a dusting of cheese and serve with lemon wedges. This can be eaten warm or at room temperature.

{ **ALSO GREAT WITH:**

Asparagus or spinach—cook both just until tender, drain, and proceed as directed in step 2. }

NOTES FROM A NOVICE: VEGETABLE CRISPER CRASH

BY LUCA QUINN (my third-born son and newly emerging home cook)

It was a breezy Sunday August afternoon and I had just returned home from the gym. Post-workout hunger was kicking in, but the thought of cooking and cleaning was daunting, so I asked my mom if any food had been cooked.

She responded, "No, but I'm going to make a stir-fry. Can you mince garlic and ginger for me?" I quickly agreed, and she showed me how to peel ginger (using the rounded tip of a small spoon to scrape the skin off), which became another notch on my belt of simple cooking preparation techniques. I realized (admittedly, rather slowly) that my mom was Tom Sawyering me into making my own lunch, as I progressed from the garlic-ginger mince to slicing the scallions to taking charge of the whole thing. "I'll just let you do it," she faux-casually said as she took a seat in the kitchen.

I couldn't reasonably object. I had never cooked stir-fry before, let alone used a wok. But to my relief, I had the best coach in my corner, advising my every move. It was time to chop up the veggies: broccoli, carrots, and collards—what we like to call a true "fridge dive."

I learned during this process that once the cooking begins, it's fast and hectic, so be prepared! Have everything prechopped. (Cut the vegetables in similar sizes, like small broccoli florets and carrot coins, so they can cook together in harmony and all end up nicely tender when finished.) Plan the order in which you're going to put the ingredients in the pan. My mom mutters, "High heat. High heat. High heat. Let the wok get scalding hot before you put anything in." She means so hot that you can't even hover over it.

Another rule when using a wok: cook in small batches! You want to cook everything evenly, and if the wok is overcrowded, your stir-fry will cook unevenly.

We decided to go Korean-style at the end with a fried egg on top and the stir-fry spooned over a bed of leftover rice (it's a constant in our house). In my opinion, the best part about this dish was the crispy rice—what my Korean best friend has told me is called nurungii—that sticks to the wok as you're cooking.

basic veg stir-fry

Pour in some oil. Ginger (okay to leave it out if you don't have it), garlic, and scallion get thrown in first, but don't let them sit or they will burn. Continuously stir. After a few seconds (not even a whole minute), chopped green beans or zucchini, sliced bok choy, and shredded carrots get thrown in. Each vegetable goes in according to how long it takes to cook—obviously the longest goes in first. This entire cooking process is accompanied by vigorous stirring, flipping, and shaking of the wok. Keep it moving. Add a little water to steam the veggies as they cook. If you are using rice, toss it in after the veggies are softened up. Next up, fish sauce. I call this the game changer, adding flavor that salt can't begin to achieve—but not fishy flavor. Serve with a sprinkling of toasted sesame seeds and a citrus wedge.

indian-spiced cauliflower and carrots

serves 6

At almost every meal, I like to serve a couple of vegetables. The more you switch up your offerings and try to keep them interesting, the easier it is to influence vegetable-eating habits (in people of all ages—I still meet grown men who unapologetically say they don't like vegetables!). In this recipe, a quasi-exotic spice mix, contrasting colors, and varying shapes elevate these otherwise ordinary vegetables. If you don't have turmeric and coriander, you can omit them or substitute a couple of teaspoons of curry powder. You can make this as spicy, garlicky, or mellow as you like depending on the balance of the ingredients. Experiment until you find some mixtures you like.

THE SEASONING PASTE

2 inches of fresh ginger, peeled and roughly chopped

3 garlic cloves

1 tablespoon vegetable oil

2 teaspoons ground coriander

1½ teaspoons coarse salt

1 teaspoon ground turmeric

¼ teaspoon cayenne pepper, or to taste

2 tomatoes, cored and chopped

1 head cauliflower, separated into small florets and stem sliced

5 or 6 carrots, cut on the bias into ¾-inch-thick pieces

½ cup water

1 To make the seasoning paste, purée the ginger, garlic, and oil in a blender or food processor. Heat a large skillet over high heat. Add the ginger mixture and sauté for 30 seconds. Stir in the coriander, salt, turmeric, and cayenne. Sauté for 2 minutes more.

2 Stir in the tomatoes to incorporate, about a minute. Add the cauliflower and carrots, stirring to coat with the seasonings. Add the water. Cover, reduce the heat to medium, and cook until the vegetables are tender, about 10 minutes.

WAYS WITH THIS SEASONING PASTE

Rice: toast 1 cup rice in a bit of oil or butter, add the seasoning paste, and stir to cook for a couple of minutes. Add 1½ cups water or chicken broth and simmer, covered, for 20 minutes.

Shrimp: coat peeled shrimp with the paste and marinate for 30 minutes. Place on skewers and grill until cooked through, 2 minutes per side.

Chickpeas: drain and rinse a can of chickpeas. Cook the seasoning paste for a few minutes with a tablespoon of tomato paste. Add the chickpeas and ½ cup water. Simmer until heated through. Top with chopped fresh cilantro.

steamed yet crispy string beans

serves 4 to 6

Green beans are one of the things that shows up a lot in my family's vegetable rotation, and switching up the style keeps them interesting. Green beans feel like one of the more "meaty" vegetables (especially with the addition of thinly sliced prosciutto!), so I use this as a side with a vegetarian pasta or meatless main.

1 pound haricots verts or green beans, halved lengthwise

1½ to 2 tablespoons olive oil

4 slices prosciutto, ham, or salami, thinly sliced crosswise

3 jarred roasted red peppers, drained and minced

½ teaspoon coarse salt

¼ teaspoon crushed red pepper flakes

1 Bring ¼ inch of water to a boil in a large skillet. Add the beans, cover, and steam until tender, 3 to 4 minutes. Drain the beans and wipe the pan clean.

2 Heat the skillet over medium heat. Swirl in 1 tablespoon of the oil. When it shimmers, add the prosciutto and sauté until crispy, about 2 minutes. Transfer to a paper towel. Swirl some more oil in the same skillet and add the roasted peppers. Cook just until heated through, about 1 minute.

3 Add the beans, salt, and red pepper flakes to the pan and toss to combine. Top with the crispy prosciutto.

CHERRY-PICK YOUR BEANS

When green beans are well chosen, devoid of brown spots or rotting ends, they'll last in the crisper for at least 10 days. Like cherries, they can't be grabbed by huge handfuls from the produce bin and just dumped in a bag. Take the time to choose them one by one at the store (those mushy brown spots are rampantly contagious, and the damaged beans will soon infect pristine specimens). As for trimming them, you only need to snap off the vine end.

orangey basil beets

serves 4 to 6

The flavors of oranges and beets have a natural affinity for each other in a tart and sweet way. Pour the citrusy vinaigrette over the beets while they're still warm so the dressing flavors will be quickly absorbed.

3 large beets, scrubbed

Finely grated zest and juice of 1 orange

1 teaspoon red wine vinegar

¼ teaspoon coarse salt

Freshly ground black pepper

2 tablespoons extra-virgin olive oil

¼ cup fresh basil leaves, roughly torn

1 Preheat the oven to 400°F. Wrap the beets in foil and roast until tender, about 1 hour. When cool enough to handle, peel the beets and cut into ¼-inch-thick slices. Spread the slices on a platter.

2 Meanwhile, whisk together the orange zest and juice, vinegar, salt, and a couple grinds of pepper. While whisking, slowly drizzle in the oil until thickened.

3 Pour the vinaigrette over the beets and scatter the basil leaves over the top.

WAYS WITH PREPPED AND PEELED BEETS

Once the beets are cooked through step 1,
try any of these serving options:

- Layer sliced beets on a platter with sliced ripe tomatoes. Dress with olive oil and salt.

- Chop the beets into cubes and toss with a dash of white wine vinegar, a dollop of prepared horseradish, salt, a pinch of sugar, and chopped fresh dill.

- Quarter the beets and top them with fresh goat cheese or sliced blue cheese and toasted walnuts.

bread and butter pickled vegetables

makes four 8-ounce jars

Your fridge's crisper can be a maddening hotbed of betrayal: you get home from the market, drop in some cukes, and revisit them a few days later . . . to find that they've completely morphed into sweaty mush. (This is especially probable if the cucumbers are still encased in a plastic bag.) Avoid this with quick pickling—this fast process makes it so vegetables will last in your refrigerator much longer than fresh ones (up to about a month). And they are a super-satisfying, healthy snack.

1½ cups white wine vinegar

⅓ cup sugar

1 tablespoon coarse salt

2 cups water

2 medium carrots, cut into 3-inch sticks

1 red bell pepper, cut into 3-inch sticks

½ cucumber, cut into 3-inch sticks

1 In a small saucepan, combine the vinegar, sugar, salt, and water. Bring to a boil over high heat, stirring to dissolve the sugar and salt.

2 Divide the vegetables among four 8-ounce canning jars. Carefully pour the hot brine over the vegetables. Let the pickles cool before serving or putting lids on the jars. Pickled vegetables can be stored in an airtight container in the refrigerator for several weeks.

WAYS WITH PICKLED VEGETABLES

Sandwich: layer pickles on a cheesy, beefy sandwich for a crisp contrast to the creamy fattiness.

Salad: instead of fresh vegetables, add pickled vegetables to a salad of chopped romaine lettuce. Dress with olive oil alone, since the vegetables are already infused with vinegar.

Fried Chicken (page 55) or Thai Red Ribs (page 10): serve pickles in a small dish alongside the fried or smoked meat for a colorful, eye-popping acidic crunch that plays off the salty, succulent meat.

FREEZER-FRESH PRODUCE

A good selection of frozen vegetables in your freezer will allow for quick sides for dinner, as well as foods for breakfast and dessert. Using good-quality frozen veggies and fruits is often preferable to choosing an off-season fresh version.

But not all store-bought frozen foods are created equal. Many turn mushy or change texture in other ways when frozen (take cauliflower, for instance). So you won't waste dollars on some frozen produce, here's what to look for:

- Look for the words "flash frozen" (a method that retains maximum nutrients).

- The ingredient panel should list only the vegetable and water.

- Don't buy bags of "buttered" anything (you can add that at home).

- Don't invest in the steam-in-bag veggies—it's so easy to dump a bag into a microwave-safe container to steam or into a pot with a little water and cover and steam on the stovetop.

Here are some quick recipe suggestions for good frozen produce:

Sautéed corn and edamame: sauté shallots in butter. Add edamame, corn, salt, and pepper and cook until golden on the edges, about 5 minutes.

Artichoke hearts: make a vegetable casserole with these winners. Combine them with the breaded topping from the Haddock Italiano recipe (page 102), place in an oiled casserole dish, cover, and bake at 400°F for 20 minutes. Uncover and bake for an additional 15 minutes.

Peas: these are great steamed and buttered or added to Shepherd's Pie (page 38). They also are a tasty side dish for a Standing Rib Roast (page 215) and work well stirred into rice or soup.

Fruit: blueberries, raspberries, peaches, and strawberries are all good choices for the freezer. Use them in smoothies or line the bottom of a bowl with them before topping with piping-hot oatmeal. Cook them down with a little sugar and lemon juice to make a sauce for French toast, pancakes, or desserts.

fresh tomato and corn mélange

makes enough sauce for 1 pound of pasta, gnocchi, or steamed green beans

Tomatoes and corn are the perfect same-time-next-year summer lovers—they both come into abundance in mid-July and bring out the best of each other's magical flavors. Make this recipe several hours ahead of time, and the flavors will meld deeply together. Use it as a sauce for pasta, gnocchi, and green beans, or as a topping for creamy polenta. It's also a tasty relish for grilled meat, poultry, or fish.

2 pounds grape or cherry tomatoes, halved, or
2 large tomatoes, chopped

6 garlic cloves, smashed

Handful of fresh basil leaves, torn

2 tablespoons extra-virgin olive oil

1 teaspoon coarse salt

5 ears fresh sweet corn, in the husk

1 Preheat the oven to 400°F. Combine the tomatoes, garlic, basil, oil, and salt in a large bowl.

2 Meanwhile, place the unshucked ears of corn in the oven and roast for about 20 minutes (you'll smell the aroma of sweet corn when they're done). Let the corn cool in the husks. Remove the husks and shave the kernels off the cobs into the tomato mixture. Stir and use as desired (this can be done several hours in advance).

LIVESAVER LESSON

YOU DON'T HAVE TO SHUCK THE CORN!

It started in childhood, when my chore was shucking the corn, and my grandmother barked at me if I didn't remove every strand of silk. It grew into a compulsive need to strip the ears perfectly, until one summer afternoon when I was just too tired and decided to experiment. I cooked the whole cobs—husks and all—in the oven. After 20 minutes, not only was the corn cooked, but the husk and every last strand of silk came off without any fuss! (This technique also works on a covered grill.)

LEAFY GREENS

Cooked greens at dinner are a Quinn family habit. We never gave the kids the option of saying no; greens were just always on their plate, night after night, nestled next to pasta, beans, or chicken. It might have been cooked cabbage, kale, Swiss chard, spinach, escarole, bok choy, or collards.

Just like each of my sons, each green has its own personality and challenges. While escarole's water-filled leaves shrink down to almost nothing when cooked, what's left behind has a soft, subtle, gently bitter, almost feminine flavor. With both escarole and spinach, you must start with way more raw leaves than you think you'll need because they cook down so much. Kale, on the other hand, is sturdy and muscular, and its natural sugars easily caramelize in sizzling olive oil. It requires no coddling.

I declare with total anecdotal certainty that eating cooked greens contributes to an overall feeling of wellness. If I feel a little queasy— maybe I've eaten too much sugar or rich food—greens will quell that discomfort. I inhale them and feel better immediately.

Once you begin to fill your meals with well-cooked greens, you'll start to crave more. Try to expand your horizons, too. The next time you're at the grocery store or farmers' market, pick up the bunch that looks the most interesting, appealing, or unusual. Clean them by actually submerging them in a sink or large bowl filled with cold water and repeating this as many times as it takes to rid them of any grit (don't rely on rinsing alone). This is such an important step, especially when you're trying to make the case for greens to reluctant potato-favorers. Nothing will turn off a timid vegetable eater faster than chomping down into gritty greens! And finally, savor the stems. The stalky ends of broccoli rabe, collards, or Swiss chard can be peeled and/or finely sliced and then cooked with the leaves.

barely touched spinach

serves 4

The key to cooking crave-worthy spinach is watching the pot: Never take your eye off the delicate leaves as they cook to the perfect tender-yet-sturdy texture while still holding their juices. This is my number one side dish for Spaghetti and Simple Tomato Sauce (page 120), and I love to serve it with Small Steamed New Potatoes (page 175) alongside Trout with Almonds (page 98).

2 tablespoons unsalted butter

2 pounds baby or young spinach leaves, or the freshest available, gently washed and drained

Pinch of freshly grated nutmeg (optional)

Coarse salt

1 Heat a straight-sided 3-quart pan over high heat. Swirl in 1 tablespoon of the butter. Add the spinach, bit by bit, waiting until the most recent addition collapses and makes room before adding the next batch. Stir in the nutmeg.

2 After the last addition of leaves, cook for 1 minute more (the leaves should be collapsed but still shapely; if using more mature leaves, allow more cooking time). Stir in the remaining 1 tablespoon butter, season with salt, and serve warm.

garlicky collard greens

serves 8 to 10

This comes straight from my Brazilian friend Michelli, who dissects and prepares the collards like a surgeon. She does not use the stalks at all, and finely shreds the leaves. This helps both the cooking and the flavor, since there's more surface area to soak up the yummy garlicky oil.

3 bunches collard greens (about 3 pounds)

¼ cup extra-virgin olive oil

9 garlic cloves, minced

¼ teaspoon coarse salt, plus more for seasoning

1 Cut out the stems and center ribs of the collard greens, keeping the leaves whole. Clean the greens thoroughly by submerging them in a bowl or sink of water. Lift out and repeat the process until the greens are grit-free, then stack them, still wet, starting with larger leaves on the bottom. Tightly roll stacks of leaves lengthwise, like a cigar. Slice crosswise as thinly as possible.

2 Heat the oil and garlic together in a large skillet over medium heat, stirring until the garlic is golden brown, 2 to 3 minutes. Add the collard greens, folding with tongs so the garlic gets tossed with the greens and they start to wilt, about 1 minute. Add the salt and continue folding until the greens have all wilted and begin to release their moisture, 2 to 3 minutes. Transfer the collards to a serving bowl. Season with salt to taste and serve.

braised cabbage

serves 6

While any cabbage can be used for this dish, I especially love the texture and flavor of good old-fashioned, standard-issue, hyper-affordable green cabbage. It yields at least 8 cups of cooked veg and makes an awesome platform for fried eggs the next day. Or mash the cabbage with potatoes for a version of the Irish dish Colcannon (page 178).

1 tablespoon olive or vegetable oil

1 onion, chopped

2 fresh green chilies, such as serrano or jalapeño, minced

4 strips bacon, chopped (optional)

1 small cabbage, cored and shredded

2 or 3 small carrots, finely chopped

½ teaspoon coarse salt

½ cup chicken broth or water

1 Heat a large skillet over high heat. Swirl in the oil. When it shimmers, add the onions, chilies, and bacon. While stirring, sauté until the bacon starts to turn golden brown and the onions begin to caramelize, 3 to 5 minutes.

2 Add the cabbage, carrots, and salt and stir to combine. Pour in the broth or water, reduce the heat to medium-low, and continue to cook, stirring occasionally, until the cabbage is tender, about 15 to 20 minutes. Add a small amount of water if needed to avoid scorching.

CABBAGE IS KING OF THE CRISPER

There is no vegetable that can languish in your crisper as long as cabbage and still survive to produce a totally pleasing vegetable dish. The tightly overlapping layers of hearty, smooth leaves are like nature's version of Saran Wrap and keep the underlying leaves fresh longer than you could reasonably expect. Peel off and discard any leaves that do go a little limp and mangy, until you reach the sturdy, firm, usable parts.

shredded brussels sprouts and kale

serves 6 to 8

These two vegetables have similar characteristics, yet slightly different textures and tastes. When cooked together, the result is a bittersweet side dish that makes a robust counterpoint to Tangy Grilled and Glazed Salmon (page 105). I like to use lacinato kale, which is also called *cavolo nero* (black kale) or Tuscan or dinosaur kale, and is used in many Italian dishes.

1 pound Brussels sprouts

1 pound lacinato kale or common kale

¼ cup olive oil

2 shallots, halved lengthwise and thinly sliced crosswise

1½ teaspoons coarse salt

⅛ teaspoon crushed red pepper flakes

2 tablespoons mild vinegar, such as white wine, champagne, or rice

1 Trim the ends of the Brussels sprouts and shred in a food processor or finely slice. Trim the kale, removing the thick center stems, and thinly slice the leaves.

2 Heat the oil in a large, straight-sided sauté pan over medium-high heat. When the oil shimmers, add the shallots and cook until they begin to soften and sweat, about 1 minute.

3 Add the shredded Brussels sprouts, kale, salt, and red pepper flakes to the pan and cook, stirring occasionally, until the vegetables are wilted and tender, about 5 to 10 minutes. Stir in the vinegar, remove from the heat, and serve.

DROOLICIOUS

squash gnocchi with sage butter

serves 4 to 6

This recipe came into being when the calamitous Superstorm Sandy hit the East Coast and grocery shopping was all but impossible in my neighborhood. A butternut squash that had been sitting around on the counter came in handy, especially since all that's needed to make gnocchi (besides squash or potatoes) is some flour and salt. Sage was growing outside and there was butter in the freezer.

1 winter squash, such as butternut or acorn, quartered and seeded (about 2 pounds)

2 cups all-purpose flour, plus more as needed

1 tablespoon coarse salt, plus more as needed

1 cup (2 sticks) unsalted butter

5 sprigs fresh sage, leaves removed

Freshly grated Parmesan cheese, for serving

Freshly ground black pepper

1) Preheat the oven to 375°F. Place the squash in a baking dish along with ¼ inch of water. Cover with foil and bake until soft throughout, about 40 minutes. When cool enough to handle, scoop the flesh from the skin into a large bowl, mash it until smooth, and let cool (this is important because hot squash sucks up flour, which makes for leaden gnocchi).

2) Whisk together the flour and salt in a separate bowl. Slowly add the dry ingredients to the cooled squash, using your hands to combine completely, until the dough pulls away from your hands in a soft mass. Add more flour as necessary to achieve the desired consistency (which should resemble a rough pizza dough).

3) Sprinkle some flour on a clean work surface. Separate the dough into several pieces and roll each into a log the size and shape of a large cigar. Cut each "cigar" into 1-inch pieces. To form the gnocchi, dip a fork in flour, and then place the tines on top of a piece of dough. Applying medium pressure, gently roll the gnocchi toward you with the fork, releasing pressure gradually as you roll, until it is completely rolled off the tines (repeatedly flour the fork to prevent

sticking). Repeat with each piece of dough, placing the finished gnocchi on a floured baking sheet. (You can use your thumb instead of a fork if desired.) The gnocchi should resemble tiny footballs with a cup in the center.

4 Bring a large pot of salted water to a boil. When it boils, heat a large skillet over medium-high heat and swirl in the butter. Add the sage leaves and cook until lightly crisp. Stir to coat them in butter.

Meanwhile, drop about 8 gnocchi into the boiling water at a time and cook until they float to the surface, 2 to 3 minutes. Remove with a slotted spoon and add directly to the sage butter. Toss to coat the gnocchi in the butter. Repeat the process with the remaining gnocchi. Add up to ½ cup of the gnocchi cooking water to the sage butter to make a pan sauce. Serve in shallow bowls, spooning some sage butter sauce over each serving. Sprinkle with Parmesan and a couple grinds of black pepper.

EVEN KIDS CAN MAKE GNOCCHI

Making gnocchi is an excellent kitchen project to do with kids. Not only is it the closest they are ever going to come to eating Play-Doh and getting away with it, but it's practically impossible to screw up. Little hands can do the rolling and a dull plastic knife can be used to cut the small pieces before shaping. Once your little dumplings get a taste of the little dumplings they've made, doused in a buttery sauce, they'll remember it forever—and may well be hooked on cooking.

eggplant rollatini

serves 6 to 8

This is one of those recipes tucked inside many Italian grandmas' recipe boxes that is worthy of a modern meal. The thinly sliced and rolled eggplants melt with the cheese and savory ham and bubble away in a tangy red sauce that hits the spot for any generation. The whole recipe can be prepared up to several hours in advance and baked when you're ready. Just allow enough time for it to cool before serving so that the liquids from the sauce and cheese are reabsorbed into each piece. (Omit the prosciutto for a vegetarian version.)

2 cups fresh ricotta cheese

3 tablespoons grated Parmesan cheese, plus more for sprinkling

1 to 1½ pounds fresh mozzarella cheese

1 large egg

½ teaspoon coarse salt

⅛ teaspoon freshly ground black pepper

¼ cup olive oil

2 large eggplants, peeled and cut lengthwise into twelve ¼-inch-thick slices

8 ounces sliced prosciutto or ham (optional)

2 to 3 cups Simple Tomato Sauce (page 120)

1 loaf Italian bread, for serving

1 In a large bowl, combine the ricotta and the Parmesan cheese. Shred enough mozzarella to measure ½ cup and add it to the bowl; reserve the remaining mozzarella. Add the egg, salt, and pepper and mix well.

2 Heat a large skillet on medium-high heat. Swirl in the oil. When it shimmers, fry the eggplant slices in batches until they are flexible enough for rolling, about 3 minutes per side. (Alternatively, the eggplants can be roasted in a 400°F oven: Brush the slices with oil and place on a baking sheet. Roast for 20 minutes, flipping the eggplants halfway through cooking.)

3 Drain the eggplants on paper towels and let cool for about 10 minutes. Spread a thin layer of the ricotta mixture on a piece of eggplant. Top it with a slice of prosciutto, if using. Roll the eggplant into a rollatini. Repeat with the remaining eggplant slices and filling.

4 Preheat the oven to 400°F. Coat the bottom of a deep baking dish with some of the tomato sauce. Place the rollatini in the dish, nestling them close to each other. When the pan is filled, put some sauce on the top of the eggplants and sprinkle with Parmesan. Finally, cut slices from the remaining fresh mozzarella and place on top of each rollatini. Bake until the cheese is melted and bubbling, about 20 minutes. Let rest for at least 10 minutes before serving with slices of Italian bread.

eggplant parmesan

serves 8

Like many Italian grandmothers, mine taught me to make eggplant parm by coating eggplant with seasoned flour, eggs, and bread crumbs, frying the slices in olive oil, and then layering them with plenty of cheese and sauce. But frying all those eggplant slices is such a pain (and they suck up so much oil) that I created this updated version. It skips most of the oil—and the time needed to stand over a hot, splattering pan—but still delivers that longed-for crusty, cheesy eggplant flavor.

4 medium eggplants (about 1 pound each), sliced crosswise into ⅔-inch-thick slices

Coarse salt

2 tablespoons extra-virgin olive oil

4 garlic cloves, minced

Two 28-ounce cans whole tomatoes, pulsed in a blender

½ teaspoon crushed red pepper flakes

6 cups fresh bread crumbs

2 cups grated Parmesan cheese, plus more for topping

4 large eggs

2 cups all-purpose flour

Freshly ground black pepper

Two 8-ounce balls fresh mozzarella, sliced

1 Season the eggplant slices all over with salt and arrange on two baking sheets. To make the tomato sauce: heat a large saucepan over medium-high heat. Swirl in the oil. When it shimmers, add the garlic and sauté, stirring, for 30 seconds. Stir in the tomatoes and red pepper flakes. Simmer for 30 minutes.

2 Combine the bread crumbs and cheese in a shallow dish. Whisk the eggs with a pinch of salt in another dish. Spread the flour in a third dish. Using a clean cloth towel or paper towel, press down on both sides of the eggplant slices to remove the moisture created by the salting process. Ready a couple of clean baking sheets (top with a wire cooling rack if you can) before beginning the breading process.

3 Preheat the oven to 400°F. Using a fork or tongs, dip each slice of eggplant (on both sides) in the flour, then in the eggs, and finally the bread crumbs. Lay each piece on the baking sheets and let the breaded slices rest to dry out for 10 to 15 minutes. Bake until a deep golden crust forms, 30 to 40 minutes. Reduce the heat to 375°F.

4 Spread a thin layer of the tomato sauce on the bottom of a 9-by-13-inch baking pan. Arrange some of the eggplant slices to cover the bottom of the pan. Top each piece of eggplant with 1 slice of mozzarella and then spoon a little tomato sauce over the mozzarella. Continue layering with the remaining ingredients. Spoon a thin layer of tomato sauce over the top layer and sprinkle with Parmesan cheese and freshly ground pepper. Drizzle with oil and bake until golden brown and bubbling, 30 to 35 minutes.

EGGPLANT IS THE MEAT OF THE VEGETABLE WORLD

Eggplant can be a polarizing vegetable, especially in my family. My husband has long maligned it openly to our boys, calling it the organ meat of vegetables. This hasn't turned them off completely, but it's certainly not the first vegetable they ask for. In Middle Eastern cultures, eggplant is like a meat, in that it delivers the texture and bulk in many a meal. I've recently been leading a little eggplant rebellion, cooking a lot more of it for my family and getting them to see the light of how good it can be.

Granted, it can be a tricky plant to approach: a large purple-skinned bulb doesn't exactly suggest a quick-cooking technique, like, say, a steak does. And yet, when sliced lengthwise, it's a perfect meat-like substitute for steak. Slice it crosswise, and it's a vegetable stand-in for a burger. The key is to tame the cottony white flesh, which sops up seemingly endless tablespoons of oil. Many recipes call for slicing the eggplant (the common large purple variety) and salting the pieces. Unless you are using baby eggplant, this is a good practice. It not only calms any bitterness, but it helps the eggplant slices resist the absorption of oil during cooking. If you salt the flesh, it sweats out liquid, which should be blotted off with a towel. What remains is a damp film that repels oil.

When sliced and cooked on high heat for enough time, eggplant develops a beautifully caramelized skin. Take care to cook it long enough so that the flesh inside becomes soft, creamy, and tender. Nothing is more off-putting than having that undercooked, wet towel texture in the final dish, not to mention a bitter, oddly metallic flavor.

baba ghanoush

Roast or char a whole eggplant, uncovered, over a flame or in a 450°F oven (prick the skin first) for about 20 minutes to achieve a silky, smoky-flavored flesh. Remove the skin, chop the interior, and mix it with tahini, lemon juice, garlic, and salt.

zucchini fritters

makes 8 to 10 fritters

"Meatless Monday" was an uphill battle with my family. Intellectually, they could understand its benefits for their health, the planet, and our wallets; they just preferred to discuss those things over a nice juicy burger. I eventually won them over with this all-veg recipe, which delivers big with satisfying flavor. This makes a great vegetarian main dish with My Mujadara (page 134) or a side dish with Middle Eastern Stuffed Lamb Roll (page 221) or Tangy Grilled and Glazed Salmon (page 105).

2 zucchini, grated (about 2 cups)

3 scallions, finely chopped

¼ cup chopped fresh dill

2 tablespoons chopped fresh mint leaves

½ teaspoon coarse salt

¼ teaspoon freshly ground black pepper

⅓ cup all-purpose flour

⅓ cup crumbled feta cheese

1 large egg, beaten

1 tablespoon extra-virgin olive oil

Plain yogurt, for serving

1 lemon, cut into wedges, for serving

1 In a large bowl, combine the zucchini, scallions, dill, mint, salt, and pepper. Stir in the flour, feta, and egg.

2 Heat a large skillet over medium-high heat. Swirl in the oil. When it shimmers, drop ¼-cup scoops of the mixture into the pan, spacing them as evenly as you can and working in batches if necessary. Lightly press down on each fritter with a spoon. Cook, flipping halfway through, until cooked through and lightly golden brown around the edges, 12 to 15 minutes. Serve the fritters drizzled with yogurt and with lemon wedges on the side.

WAYS WITH GRATED ZUCCHINI

For a delectable pasta sauce or topping for bruschetta, heat a large skillet over high heat, swirl in some olive oil, and add a couple of grated zucchini, a minced garlic clove, and a large pinch of salt. Cook, stirring continuously, until the moisture has evaporated and you have a caramelized, paste-like sauce. Toss with cooked pasta or spoon onto toasted bread and top with grated Parmesan cheese.

zucchini and potatoes jambot

serves 4 to 6

This southern Italian peasant dish is a rustic (yet inspired) pairing of hearty and toothsome potatoes that make a sturdy filling for the soft butteriness of cooked zucchini. My family has cooked this dish for three generations (that I know of), and I like to serve it with Broiled Black Pepper Sirloin Steak (page 28) or Hot and Crispy Fried Chicken (page 55). If there are any leftovers, I put an egg on it in the morning, natch.

¼ cup extra-virgin olive oil

1 tablespoon unsalted butter

1 small yellow onion, chopped

2 large or 4 small potatoes, cut into cubes

Coarse salt

2 medium or 4 small zucchini, cut into cubes (a little smaller than the potato cubes)

Freshly ground black pepper

1 teaspoon dried Italian seasoning (or dried oregano and/or thyme)

Chopped fresh parsley leaves, for serving (optional)

Heat the oil and butter in a 12-inch straight-sided skillet over medium-high heat. Add the onions and cook until they start to soften, about 2 minutes. Add the potatoes and a pinch of salt and cook for 10 minutes, stirring occasionally. Add the zucchini, pepper, Italian seasoning, and ¾ teaspoon salt. Sauté until the zucchini and potatoes are just tender but not mushy, 8 to 10 minutes. Serve, garnished with parsley, if you like.

small steamed new potatoes

serves 2

New potatoes taste like magic—as if you reached into the dirt and pulled out sweet butter. This recipe, in which I steam those little golden orbs, lets their simple beauty shine through. I love the combination of fish and potatoes, especially when the spuds are nestled up next to Barely Touched Spinach (page 161) and Trout with Almonds (page 98). *Photo on page 99.*

Coarse salt

7 to 10 small yellow new potatoes

1 tablespoon unsalted butter

2 tablespoons chopped fresh herbs, such as parsley, tarragon, or thyme

¼ teaspoon freshly ground white pepper

1 Put 1 cup water and some salt into a saucepan fitted with a steamer basket and bring to a boil.

2 Add the potatoes to the basket and steam until they are knife-tender and the water has evaporated, about 20 minutes.

3 Transfer the potatoes to a bowl and add the butter, herbs, and white pepper. Toss to coat. Serve warm.

BOILED POTATOES LOVE BUTTERMILK

Here is a glorious yet unexpected way to serve steamed or boiled potatoes: once cooked, place the potatoes in a bowl and pour about ½ cup buttermilk over them. The creamy, cool acidity of the liquid tastes delicious with the soft texture and warmth of the potatoes.

sautéed potatoes and poblano peppers

makes 2 cups

Pick a purpose for this recipe and it will not disappoint. This speedy mixture can be a vegetarian filling for tacos, a side dish, a sauce for grilled steak or pork chops, or a tidy little base for a fried or poached egg.

Coarse salt

2 potatoes, peeled and chopped

4 poblano peppers

1 tablespoon vegetable oil

1 onion, sliced

1 Boil a pot of salted water. Add the potatoes and cook until tender, 15 to 18 minutes. Drain.

2 Meanwhile, roast the chilies on an open flame, rotating as each part chars, until the skin is totally blackened, about 7 minutes. (Alternatively, place the peppers on a baking sheet and broil, rotating to achieve the overall charring.) Place the roasted chilies into a plastic bag and let

them steam for about 15 minutes. When cool enough to handle, remove 1 pepper at a time from the bag and peel or rub off the skin. Remove and discard the core, ribs, and seeds. Tear the flesh into strips and set aside.

3 Heat a large skillet over medium-high heat. Swirl in the oil. When it shimmers, add the onions and potatoes and sauté until tender, about 8 minutes.

4 Add the chili strips and ½ teaspoon salt. Stir to combine and cook, covered, until the onions and potatoes are golden on the edges, about 5 minutes.

ABOUT POBLANOS

Originating from Pueblo, a state in central Mexico, poblanos are one of the most ubiquitous chilies in Mexican cooking (for instance, they are often stuffed for chilies rellenos). This mild chili is longer and thinner than a bell pepper, and the dark green skin is almost always removed before eating (usually after roasting so that the skins can be peeled effortlessly). While more and more markets carry poblanos, they can be substituted with either Anaheim or Hatch chilies. When dried, poblanos turn red and are known as ancho chilies.

colcannon

serves 6

Also known as stamp, colcannon turns potatoes and greens into a full and hearty meal. I like to use cabbage, kale, collards—whatever leftover greens I have. A layer of caramelized fried onion tops the buttery-soft potato mountain.

8 tablespoons (1 stick) unsalted butter

2 onions, sliced

6 potatoes, or 5 to 6 cups leftover mashed potatoes

Coarse salt

1 cup milk, warmed

Freshly ground black pepper

2 cups leftover cooked greens such as cabbage, kale, or collards (page 162)

1 Melt 3 tablespoons of the butter in a large skillet over medium-high heat. Add the onions and cook until they are golden and caramelized, 15 to 20 minutes.

2 Meanwhile (if starting with raw potatoes), boil the potatoes in salted boiling water until tender, 10 to 20 minutes. Drain, reserving 1 cup of the cooking water. Peel and discard the skins and mash the potatoes with the milk and 2 tablespoons of the butter. If the potatoes are too thick, add some of the cooking water to achieve a smooth consistency. Season the potatoes with salt and pepper. Stir in the cooked greens. Melt the remaining 3 tablespoons butter. To serve, place a mound of potatoes and greens in a shallow bowl and make a well in the center. Fill with some melted butter and top with some of the fried onions.

LOVE A GOOD MASH

When there are just a few potatoes, plus maybe a sweet potato or some carrots in the kitchen, it's time for a mash. Peel and boil whatever you have until tender. Drain, reserving some cooking water. Add some dairy or nut milk, reserved cooking water, salt, and pepper and mash to a rough texture. This is an amazing platform or plate-neighbor for pork chops.

To really boost the flavor, throw a couple of garlic cloves in with the boiling potatoes. They soften in the water so that they smash up beautifully with the potatoes and add a lovely, mysterious note.

baked sweet potatoes

makes 4

Someone, somewhere along the line, told me that, given how nutritious, digestion-friendly, and delicious they are, sweet potatoes should be your first and your last food in this world. I do agree that a properly roasted sweet potato is as good as food can be. Bake it long enough so that the darkly caramelized juices come oozing out.

4 large sweet potatoes

4 tablespoons (½ stick) unsalted butter

1 teaspoon coarse salt

¼ teaspoon freshly ground black pepper

1 Preheat the oven to 375°F with the rack in the middle position. Pierce the sweet potatoes all over with the tines of a fork and bake directly on the oven rack until soft and caramelized, about 1½ hours. (Place a baking sheet or large piece of aluminum foil on the rack beneath the potatoes to catch any drippings.)

2 Slash open the tops of the potatoes with the tip of a sharp knife and push the ends toward each other to open. Divide the butter, salt, and pepper among the potatoes and serve.

GREAT TOPPED WITH:

Asian twist: edamame ★ a drizzle of soy sauce ★ toasted sesame seeds

Extra veg: steamed broccoli ★ a scoop of cottage cheese ★ a sprinkling of salt ★ freshly ground black pepper

Sweet & savory: butter ★ maple syrup ★ finely grated orange zest ★ a squeeze of orange juice

bacon potato salad

serves 6

Golden-sweet onions, salty bacon, earthy potatoes—each is delicious on its own, but put them together and you have one killer potato salad. Serve it to complete a meal of Honey Mustard–Glazed Wings (page 58) or Grilled Strip Steak with Herb Butter (page 31).

Coarse salt

8 Yukon Gold potatoes, peeled and halved

1 tablespoon red wine vinegar

1 teaspoon vegetable oil

6 strips bacon, chopped

½ large white onion, chopped (about 1 cup)

3 celery stalks, sliced

¾ cup sour cream or plain Greek yogurt

½ cup mayonnaise

1 tablespoon prepared horseradish

Freshly ground black pepper

1 cup chopped fresh parsley leaves

1 In a large pot filled with salted water, boil the potatoes until tender, about 20 minutes. Drain and chop the potatoes into ¾-inch chunks. Place them in a large bowl and stir in the vinegar while the potatoes are still hot.

2 Meanwhile, heat a saucepan over medium-high heat. Swirl in the oil. When it shimmers, add the bacon and onions and sauté until the bacon is slightly crisp and the onions are golden, 8 to 10 minutes. Remove the bacon-onion mixture from the fat and add to the potatoes along with the celery.

3 In a small bowl, whisk together the sour cream, mayonnaise, and horseradish. Stir the dressing into the potatoes. Season with salt and pepper. Add the parsley and stir to combine. Cool, cover, and refrigerate until ready to serve.

princely potatoes

serves 6

I'm not going to insult you by pretending there's a health angle here. Sometimes, the mind/body just wants a dish of unapologetically fattening deliciousness—and that's where these potatoes, cooked in the classic "dauphinoise" style, come in. I like them with the Duck Breast a l'Orange (page 69) or Flat Roast Citrus Chicken (page 52).

3 pounds potatoes, such as russet, peeled and thinly sliced (about ⅛ inch thick)

1 tablespoon unsalted butter, softened

2½ cups heavy cream

1½ cups whole milk

1 garlic clove, smashed

5 ounces Gruyère cheese, shredded

1 teaspoon coarse salt

¼ teaspoon freshly ground white pepper

⅛ teaspoon freshly grated nutmeg

1 Put the peeled sliced potatoes in a bowl of cold water. Preheat the oven to 350°F with the rack in the middle position. Spread the butter across the bottom and up the sides of a 2-quart baking dish.

2 Bring the cream, milk, and garlic to a simmer in a saucepan. Drain the potatoes well and lay a quarter of them in the baking dish. Set aside 2 ounces of the cheese. Scatter a quarter of the remaining cheese over the potatoes and top with a quarter each of the salt, white pepper, and nutmeg. Pour a quarter of the cream mixture over the potatoes to just cover. Repeat with the remaining ingredients to make a total of four layers. Cover with foil, set the baking dish on a rimmed baking sheet, and bake until tender and bubbly, 40 to 45 minutes.

3 Increase the oven temperature to 400°F. Uncover the pan and top with the reserved 2 ounces cheese. Bake, uncovered, until the cheese is melted and light golden brown, about 15 minutes. Remove the dish from the oven and let rest for at least 15 minutes before serving.

ABOUT POTATOES

The distinctions between spud varieties are more than skin deep—they usually have something to do with starch content.

Russets (sometimes known as Idaho potatoes) have a high starch content, making for light and fluffy mashed potatoes. They are dry and porous and will hold their shape when baked in a gratin, even while absorbing liquid.

Yukon Golds have a medium starch content and are ideal for steaming or roasting. Their waxiness holds the pieces together and maintains their firmness or "bite," perfect for potato salad or soup.

Red potatoes fall somewhere between waxy and starchy. They will also hold their shape when steamed or boiled but are not the ideal choice for baking (roasting) with liquids. The thin skin is tender to eat.

KILLER SALADS

OPPOSITE: Watercress, Fennel, and Orange Salad (page 195)

SALAD SAVIOR

Being a mom to boys has made me a better salad maker. From a young age, girls are conditioned—by both internal and external forces—to eat salad, to accept it as a part of our gotta-stay-slim routine. Guys feel no such pressure. If a salad has even the slightest whiff of obligation, it turns into penance—and it will not be eaten. Not only will *that* particular salad go uneaten, but the boy in question will be disinclined to eat salad the next time around. One bad salad is all it takes to lose a potential greens eater, which is a shame because there are so many glorious things about salad!

The simplest ingredients can become a marvel to behold: cold crispy lettuce, a peppery olive oil, a hint of tangy vinegar, and a dusting of salt and freshly ground pepper. The key is to make sure every vegetable is cut correctly—you don't want giant chunks that sink to the bottom of the bowl. Shred, chop, or dice so that the supporting vegetables nestle among the lettuce leaves, commingling in every bite. For instance, I love the addition of mild onion—not a thick odiferous bangle but a julienned scallion or very thinly sliced mild red onion. Better yet, fry a few shallots to put on top. Heaven.

And be thoughtful when you decide to make a salad—less can be more, so don't feel compelled to concoct a crazy mix of every odd vegetable left in the crisper (and don't overdress it to compensate for its offbeat composition). Think about how the salad will complement what else is being served with the meal—or if it's the meal itself. In the case of the latter, please don't tell your sons. They'll eat a good salad as long as they do not know it's the main event. Not even the delicious Lentil Salad (page 200), which I easily could live on.

market salad

serves 6

The secret to this delicious, simple salad is the lettuce: the cooler and drier the leaves, the better the salad tastes. First, thoroughly wash the leaves, free them from grit, and dry them well. Gently wrap the cleaned leaves in a towel, place in a loose plastic bag, and refrigerate for at least an hour (or up to 5 days) to soak up every last bit of dampness and crisp up the lettuce. When you finish it with the dressing of your choice, those dry, cold leaves will grip it beautifully.

2 small heads crisp lettuce, such as young romaine, Bibb, Boston, or red leaf, washed and dried well

Extra-virgin olive oil

Red wine vinegar

Coarse salt (preferably sea salt) and freshly ground black pepper

Tear the salad greens into a large salad bowl. Drizzle a generous bit of oil and a capful of vinegar over the top and season with salt and pepper. Toss gently to coat. Taste and add more oil, vinegar, salt, or pepper if needed.

NO DRESSING NECESSARY!

With lettuce leaves in the bowl, drizzle in a capful of olive oil at a time. (Save the vinegar for second—when you drizzle it over the salad before the oil, it just sogs up the crisp, dry leaves.) Add the vinegar next, a capful at a time, to your preferred level of tanginess. Sprinkle on some crunchy salt and roughly cracked pepper.
That's all—you don't have to overthink this.

cranberry-almond green salad with honey mustard vinaigrette

serves 4

Toasted nuts and sweet-tart dried fruit—these are the two fairy godmother ingredients that transform a plate of raw vegetables into something you are dying to eat.

1 head Boston lettuce, torn into bite-size pieces

¼ cup sliced almonds, toasted (see page 98)

¼ cup dried red cranberries

THE HONEY MUSTARD VINAIGRETTE

¾ cup olive oil

2 tablespoons freshly squeezed lemon juice

2 teaspoons Dijon mustard

½ teaspoon honey

Coarse salt and freshly ground black pepper

2 ounces blue cheese (optional)

1 Combine the lettuce, almonds, and cranberries in a large salad bowl.

2 Make the vinaigrette: In a jar with a tight-fitting lid, combine the oil, lemon juice, mustard, and honey. Cover tightly and shake well to combine and emulsify. Season with salt and pepper and shake again before serving.

3 Pour the dressing over the salad and toss to coat. Crumble blue cheese on top, if desired.

NUTS IN SALAD

Toasted nuts change the entire vibe of a salad. Whether they are sliced, chopped, or whole, their crunch and earthy flavor are the perfect counterpoints to bright, leafy greens. And the nutritional value is indisputable. There is a vast array of nuts to choose from, so experiment with toasted almonds, hazelnuts, cashews, walnuts, macadamias, pecans . . . Store your nuts in the freezer; otherwise, they will quickly turn rancid. Always taste one before using in a recipe.

ACID MAKES FOOD COME ALIVE

Vinegar and citrus juice are key components of savory flavors. A few droplets of either on your tongue kick-start your taste buds. As with salt, knowing the hows, whens, and wheres of vinegar can make the difference between dishes you crave and those that fall flat. Try to utilize different varieties of vinegar or tangy citrus juice to give each style of salad its own personality.

Red wine vinegar and **white wine vinegar** are good places to start; they will last for years, although you will use them far sooner.

Balsamic vinegar is entirely different from red and white wine vinegars. It can cook down to a robust, powerful syrup that swings easily between savory and sweet recipes (see pages 105 and 238). Take care not to overdo it, though: balsamic requires a healthy understanding and respect to avoid becoming the big flavor bully on the plate.

Conversely, **rice wine** and **champagne vinegars** are like quiet, gentle wallflowers that contribute light, beguiling notes to a dressing or marinade. They are not strong or overpowering in any way, yet still bring a mild, tangy flavor that's always welcome.

Sherry vinegar—which has gotten a lot of notice lately—acts like the well-mannered offspring of rice wine and balsamic vinegars. It has a sweet yet lightly assertive nutty taste that's understated and elegant.

Never leave the grocery store without tossing a **lemon** or **lime** into your cart. Aside from a necessary cocktail garnish, a squeeze of either along with salt and pepper dresses up a simple chicken breast, fish fillet, or ripe avocado. Lemon, lime, orange, and grapefruit juices all contribute varying levels of acidity to a salad dressing or other preparations, both in their fresh and cooked states.

kale salad

serves 6 to 8

If this recipe is discovered a hundred years from now, let it be known that it was impossible to ignore kale salad in the early decades of the twenty-first century. There's a reason a trend becomes a trend, and currently it's kale salad all the time. Once you make it yourself, it's hard to ignore its crunchy, salty, tangy appeal. The beauty of this recipe is that, unlike most salads, it benefits from being made ahead. The hearty, tenacious greens relax and soak up the lemony dressing—a to-go, packed-lunch or party salad at its best.

Finely grated zest and juice of 1 lemon, plus more juice if needed

½ teaspoon coarse salt

¼ teaspoon freshly ground black pepper

½ cup extra-virgin olive oil

1 cup grated Pecorino Romano or Parmesan cheese, or a combo of the two

1 small bunch kale, tough stems removed, leaves finely sliced crosswise (about 6 cups), chilled

1 cup sliced or slivered almonds, toasted

1. Whisk together the lemon zest and juice, salt, and pepper in a small bowl. Slowly pour in the oil, whisking continuously to emulsify the dressing.

2. Combine the kale and cheese in a large bowl. Drizzle the dressing over the salad and toss to fully coat the leaves. Press and massage the greens slightly in the process. With a wooden spoon, stir in the almonds and season with more salt and lemon juice, if needed. This recipe can be made ahead— up to 8 hours before serving.

escarole walnut salad

serves 6

If you've never worked with escarole, give this versatile green a go. When I was growing up, I was used to eating it chopped up in a soup, quickly wilted with lemon juice, or tossed into a salad. Though you can find escarole in most grocery stores, many people don't take advantage of it, perhaps because of its slight bitterness (which dissipates when cooked). In this recipe, toasted walnuts, homemade walnut oil, red wine vinegar, and shavings of Pecorino nicely balance escarole's healthful, raw intensity.

THE WALNUT DRESSING

2 cups walnuts

½ cup extra-virgin olive oil

1 garlic clove, smashed

¼ cup red wine vinegar

½ teaspoon coarse salt

¼ teaspoon freshly ground black pepper

1 head escarole, chopped

½ small red onion, thinly sliced

3 ounces Pecorino Romano cheese, shaved

1 Preheat the oven to 350°F. Spread 1 cup of the walnuts over a rimmed baking sheet and toast in the oven for 10 minutes. Turn the nuts once during roasting. Cool to room temperature and coarsely chop.

2 Finely chop the remaining 1 cup walnuts and place in a small saucepan with the olive oil and garlic. Bring to a bare simmer over medium heat. Remove the pan from the heat and set aside to cool to room temperature. When cool, strain the oil into a medium bowl and discard the nuts and garlic. Whisk in the vinegar, salt, and pepper.

3 Spread the escarole over a large platter. Sprinkle the toasted walnuts and onions over the escarole and drizzle with the dressing. Top with the shaved Pecorino Romano and serve immediately.

WAYS WITH ESCAROLE

Top a pizza: sauté escarole in olive oil with minced garlic, anchovy, and red pepper flakes.

Stir into soup: shred a handful of escarole and add to a pot of Rag Soup (page 92) instead of spinach.

With Italian sausages: after the sausages have browned and cooked through, add escarole to the pan, cover, and let the escarole wilt until tender.

chicory, red cabbage, and escarole salad

serves 6

This is the standard salad that was served at my first cooking job, a 1970s "gourmet" lunch spot that specialized in quiche and bespoke omelets. The colors and shapes of the fresh vegetables are beautiful, and there isn't a wimpy lettuce leaf in the group. Thinly sliced cabbage lends a great crunch to the curly chicory and soft escarole. I serve it on the same plate with the Egg and Ham Pie (page 90) because I like the combo of soft egg and crispy salad all in the same bite.

½ head chicory or frisée, torn into 1-inch pieces

½ small head red cabbage, thinly sliced

½ head escarole, torn into 1-inch pieces

⅓ cup extra-virgin olive oil

3 tablespoons red wine vinegar

1 teaspoon coarse salt

⅛ teaspoon freshly ground black pepper

Toss together the chicory, cabbage, and escarole in a large salad bowl. Drizzle the oil and vinegar over the greens and season with salt and pepper. Toss thoroughly and serve.

STRONG IS GOOD

All of these non-wimpy (i.e., highly flavorful and nutritious) salad leaves can be used raw in salad. Cut or tear the leaves into small pieces or shred them.

escarole ★ radicchio ★ arugula ★ chicory ★ endive ★ mustard ★ kale ★ bok choy ★ Swiss chard

watercress, fennel, and orange salad

serves 6 to 8

Crunchy, juicy, colorful—everything you look for in a salad is here. Licorice-flavored fennel, sweet orange, and earthy green watercress make a strong statement, and will add a fresh, lively component to a larger meal. *Photo on page 184.*

1 orange

2 tablespoons freshly squeezed lemon juice

½ teaspoon coarse salt

¼ teaspoon freshly ground black pepper

¼ cup extra-virgin olive oil

2 bunches watercress, trimmed

1 fennel bulb, halved lengthwise, cored, and thinly sliced

1 Hold the orange over a large salad bowl and grate the zest into the bowl. Peel and discard the remaining white pith from the orange. Holding the orange over the bowl, use a small, sharp knife to separate the orange into segments, letting the juice drip into the bowl. Set the orange segments aside. Whisk the orange zest and orange juice with the lemon juice, salt, and pepper. Add the oil in a slow, steady stream, whisking continuously.

2 Toss the watercress and fennel with the dressing just before serving. Top with the orange segments.

pizza parlor salad

serves 6

I could never understand why my guys would turn up their noses at salads I served them, yet lustily dig into the aluminum trays of salad that came with a pizza delivery. Then I decided to stop grappling—and shamelessly created a tastier facsimile at home. Here the lettuce is crisp-crunchy, devoid of any weird, unidentifiable vegetables, and doused with my mama's delicious salad dressing. *Photo on page 67.*

2 hearts of romaine, chopped

3 plum tomatoes, each cut lengthwise into 6 wedges

1 small red onion, thinly sliced into rings

½ cup pitted black olives

⅓ cup shredded Parmesan cheese

1 recipe Rose's Vinaigrette (see below)

Place the romaine on a platter and top with the tomatoes, onion, olives, and cheese. Drizzle generously with vinaigrette just before serving.

rose's vinaigrette

makes about 1 cup

1 tablespoon minced shallot or garlic

1 teaspoon Dijon mustard

1 teaspoon light brown sugar

¾ teaspoon coarse salt, or to taste

¼ teaspoon freshly ground black pepper, or to taste

¼ teaspoon Worcestershire sauce

¾ cup extra-virgin olive oil

1½ tablespoons red wine vinegar

1 tablespoon freshly squeezed lemon juice

In a clean glass jar, mash the shallot with the mustard, brown sugar, salt, pepper, and Worcestershire sauce.

Add the oil, vinegar, and lemon juice. Cover tightly and shake well to combine and emulsify. Add more salt and pepper to taste, if necessary. Use immediately or store in the refrigerator for up to 6 weeks.

great grain salad

serves 6 to 8

This salad is a gratifying meatless alternative for any robust appetite. I love to serve it alongside Kale Salad (page 191) as part of a large summer feast. You can prepare both salads in advance, which actually improves the taste when the flavors mix and meld, making both salads an ideal choice for a buffet or a portable lunch for the beach or office.

Finely grated zest and juice of 1 lemon, plus more juice if needed

2 tablespoons extra-virgin olive oil

½ teaspoon coarse salt

½ teaspoon freshly ground black pepper

3 cups cooked whole grains, such as farro, quinoa, and/or brown rice (prepared according to package instructions)

1 pint cherry tomatoes, quartered

2 scallions, thinly sliced crosswise

⅓ cup fresh herbs, such as dill, mint, basil, cilantro, or parsley, chopped

One 15-ounce can chickpeas, navy beans, or cannellini beans, drained

½ cup crumbled feta cheese, preferably Greek style

Whisk together the lemon zest and juice, salt, and pepper in a large bowl. Stir in the cooked grains (preferably when they're still warm, to better absorb the dressing), tomatoes, scallions, and herbs. Fold in the beans and feta. Adjust to taste by adding more salt, lemon juice, or oil as desired. Cover tightly with plastic wrap, and store in the refrigerator until serving, up to 3 days.

vegetable bread salad

serves 4 to 6

Everyone, everywhere, wants to eat the croutons first when they spy them in any salad, and so one based on cubed bread is especially appealing. Studding this rustic salad of colorful, familiar vegetables, the crusty bread provides an enticing reason to dig in. Serve it with carved Plain Roast Chicken (page 51) for a fierce dinner combo.

½ loaf dense, chewy Italian bread, cut into 1½-inch chunks (about 4 cups)

1 red bell pepper, cored, seeded, and chopped

1 seedless cucumber, chopped

1 tomato, cored and chopped

⅓ red onion, thinly sliced

⅔ cup extra-virgin olive oil

⅓ cup red wine vinegar

Pinch of sugar

½ teaspoon coarse salt

6 ounces feta cheese, preferably Greek style

1 Spread the bread cubes on a baking sheet and let dry out for a couple of hours or overnight—as much time as you can spare.

2 Place the bell pepper, cucumber, tomato, and onion in a bowl. Whisk together the olive oil, vinegar, sugar, and salt and pour over the vegetables. Toss to coat. Add the bread cubes and toss to combine. Allow the bread to sit for a bit to soak up the dressing.

3 Crumble the feta cheese over the salad. Cover and refrigerate until ready to serve, up to overnight.

ABOUT FETA CHEESE

Feta cheese is a great salad cheese because it crumbles nicely and brings a salty tang to cool, crisp vegetables. It's usually made from sheep's milk or a blend of sheep's and goat's milk. French-style feta is quite creamy, while the Greek style is more crumbly.

lentil salad

serves 4

The flavor and texture of lentils make them an ideal salad protein. They cook up quickly, and when tossed with vinaigrette while still warm, each little legume sucks the dressing's tang into their hearts. Serve this as a starter or as a dinner salad.

THE CROUTONS

½ loaf bread, preferably 1 day old, cut into ¾-inch cubes

3 tablespoons extra-virgin olive oil

2 garlic cloves, smashed

¼ teaspoon coarse salt

THE SALAD

1 cup lentils, preferably French

½ cup Classic French Vinaigrette (see opposite)

1 teaspoon extra-virgin olive oil

3 strips bacon, sliced crosswise into ¼-inch pieces

½ red onion, thinly sliced

¼ cup roughly chopped fresh parsley leaves

One 4-inch log mild, fresh goat cheese, sliced into 8 pieces

4 cups baby arugula

1. Make the croutons: Preheat the oven to 375°F. Toss together the bread, oil, garlic, and salt on a rimmed baking sheet. Spread out evenly and bake until golden brown, turning over a few times, about 15 minutes.

2. Meanwhile, make the salad: Place the lentils in a small saucepan and add enough water to cover by 1 inch. Bring to a boil, reduce the heat, and simmer until tender, about 15 minutes, depending on the age of the lentils. Drain, place the lentils in a large bowl, and toss with the vinaigrette while the lentils are still warm.

3. Heat a pan over medium-high heat. Swirl in the oil. When it shimmers, add the bacon and onions and sauté, stirring continuously, until the onions are soft and the bacon is crispy, about 4 minutes. Stir the bacon mixture and parsley into the lentils.

4. Divide the arugula among four plates. Spoon a quarter of the lentils over each plate of arugula, and add 2 slices of goat cheese to each. Scatter a handful of croutons over the top and serve immediately.

classic french vinaigrette

makes ¾ cup

Whip up this vinaigrette in a jar and it'll keep in the refrigerator just about indefinitely. Drizzle it over your favorite salad, a piece of grilled fish, or steamed vegetables.

½ shallot, minced

2 tablespoons freshly squeezed lemon juice

1 to 2 tablespoons red wine vinegar

1½ teaspoons Dijon mustard

Generous pinch of coarse salt

½ cup extra-virgin olive oil

Freshly ground black pepper

In a bowl or glass jar, combine the shallot, lemon juice, vinegar, mustard, and salt. Whisk together (or shake) to combine well. Slowly whisk in the olive oil. Season with salt and pepper to taste. Cover and store the bowl or jar in the refrigerator, if making ahead. Whisk or shake well before using.

HOLIDAY MEAL CIRCUIT

OPPOSITE: The Christmas Meal: Standing Rib Roast (page 215), Yorkshire Pudding (page 216), Hedgehog Potatoes (page 213), and Peas, Pearl Onions, and Mint (page 224)

CUSTOMIZE YOUR HOLIDAYS

My husband and I decided early on that we'd establish our independence around family customs during the holidays. Part of this decision was, of course, determined by economics: we simply didn't have the resources for all five of us to travel anywhere. Part of it was geographic—even if we could, our families are scattered across the United States, and visiting one side and not the other could be fraught. To be totally honest, though, most of it was about self-preservation and self-indulgence (it's the holidays, after all). When the kids were little, just getting the correct presents (and then getting them into the correct son's hands— oddly harder than it would seem), and shepherding the Santa story was labor enough. Also, two of the kids' birthdays bookend Christmas and New Year's, so for many years we were smack-dab in the middle of a potentially overwhelming vortex. So our gift to ourselves was to create the least amount of hassle and the most delicious meal—and then find a rhythm that could be replicated year after year.

Before I started hosting meals, I learned a lot as a guest. When my kids were little, we spent lots of time with my friend Meredith, who is my favorite home cook. I loved that her family was as mixed up and upside-down as mine was—no excuses, no problems, no judgment, just fun. Meredith didn't martyr herself in the kitchen. She readily asked for help, and also pounced with a skill-set-appropriate task when anyone offered it. (Not all cooks are as ready for assistance. To be a good guest, just try to be a good prep cook, and ask at least twice what you can do before accepting "Nothing, really!" as a final answer. And then, in any case, volunteer to wash dishes after dinner!) It was Meredith's husband, Lee, who taught me the life-altering art of cooking a turkey to perfection in the Weber kettle grill. I still cook our turkey outside exactly how Lee taught me to (I shared the recipe in my first book, *Mad Hungry: Feeding Men & Boys*), and this year my oldest son tended the grill alongside me.

If Thanksgiving is about grilled turkey, Christmas is about roast beef. Our meaty tradition took shape after I realized that I was surrounded by boys who were growing into men—and all they wanted was a big cut of beef. So I took a page from traditional English feasts and established a menu of standing rib roast, potatoes, Yorkshire pudding, and minted peas. Over the years, I've suggested deviating from this menu once or twice, at my own peril! There is all but an uprising if the meat and pudding are not the center of the Christmas table.

At New Year's Eve, my main concern for the past dozen or so years (since my oldest son was sixteen years old) has been cooking delicious stick-to-your-ribs food, something the boys and their friends will love to eat with us and that will be enough to fortify them as they venture out for a late-night party. I then pray that their food-filled tummies will somehow protect them from their danger-seeking selves. The past couple of years, I've stuffed and cooked a capon, my favorite poultry. With all the gravitas of a turkey, and more chicken-flavored than any chicken, it's a fine flourish to the end of yet another year.

When I was growing up, there was a lot of pageantry and symbolism around the Easter celebrations. But these days, I see this time as a new beginning for fresh ideas. We emerge from winter hibernation to sprouting green vegetation and the promise of another chance. Anything seems possible at this time of year. Foods like lamb, spinach, and rhubarb are on my mind. So is experimentation, which is heartily encouraged by my hungry boys (unlike at Christmas). I've tried all sorts of different lamb preparations over the years, but my current favorite is a Stuffed Lamb Roll (page 221), which is filled with vibrant Middle Eastern flavors.

As for so many folks over time, Thanksgiving, Christmas, New Year's, and Easter have been our gathering feast points. Whatever yours are, establish the food rituals that make you happy. Don't let anyone tell you what you have to do. Once you decide for yourself, choose carefully, because your family will want the same thing every year!

THANKSGIVING IS A FIRST FOR EVERYONE, EVERY YEAR

The Thanksgiving meal can be daunting—no matter how much experience you have in the kitchen. Even if you've prepared the bounteous meal for decades, there's always some new trend or distracting chatter that makes you question what you're doing. What kind of turkey should you get? Should you brine it? Is it okay if it's frozen—or does it need to be fresh? How big a bird do you need? And once you figure all this out, how do you choose from the zillions of recipes telling you the best route to a perfectly cooked bird? Low and slow? High and then low? Low and then high? And you haven't even started considering the stuffing, gravy, side dishes, desserts . . .

I've cooked at least twenty Thanksgiving dinners at home, and at least a dozen more at work, so here's what I've figured out along the way that will keep these nagging questions at bay:

Skip the complicated recipes. That basting brush made of sage leaves tied onto a cinnamon stick with a few chives? It is absolutely not worth it—at least not on the last Thursday of November! With each thing you make, cook it as simply as possible to get the purest flavor out of it (and to keep yourself sane). Remember, there are already many competing flavors on that plate.

Make an equipment checklist. Before you start anything, check that you have the roasting pan, twine, potholders, thermometer, cutting board, sharp knife, and turkey baster to make this whole thing happen. Make sure your oven is big enough, clean enough, and temperature-calibrated enough to pull this off. Otherwise, consider an outdoor grill for the job (full instructions in *Mad Hungry: Feeding Men & Boys*).

Brining the bird will give you some latitude. If you're shy or timid, it's harder to overcook a juiced-up bird. But it's not necessary (especially since brining a giant bird is a total pain).

Bring that bird to room temperature before cooking. That means get it out of the refrigerator way sooner than any recipe tells you to, if they tell you to at all.

Season the bird well. Use your salt with abandon. It should look like a fine layer of snow has fallen on the outside of the raw, seasoned turkey.

Stuff the darn bird. The cavity was made to flavor a big round ball of yummy, savory, flavored bread. Just be sure to cook it well.

For God's sake, use an instant-read thermometer. Spend $15 and buy a digital one. Test the leg-thigh joint until it reads 165°F (or if you are a trusting radical, 160°F). That bird *will* be cooked. Once out of the oven, the carry-over heat will continue to cook it further.

Do the backward math to get all the food on the table when you want it. Eating at midnight with a dozen drunken guests chomping at the bit is no fun. When cooking a Thanksgiving feast, prepare a production schedule ahead of time to avoid oven bumper cars, as several dishes jostle to be ready at the same time. Don't forget, once the bird has finished cooking, make sure it rests at least 20 minutes so the juices can recirculate. Don't skip this part.

Here's how you make the plan: If my bird is 18 to 20 pounds, I know it needs 3 to 4 hours of cooking, plus the 1 hour out-of-the-fridge tempering time and the time it takes to season and stuff it. Add in the resting and the carving, and figure that the turkey show must be underway 5 to 6 hours in advance of sitting down at the table to eat.

When that bird comes out of the oven, the only thing left to do is to make gravy. Sides and desserts should be all done. Make your pies on Wednesday— they will be better and easier to cut the next day.

Before you sit down to eat, clean the cooked-in kitchen. Leave no mashed potato–crusted pots in the sink. Get your pies ready (in the oven to rewarm), and set out the knife and spatula to cut and serve. Have the dessert plates and forks nearby. Make sure the whipped cream is whipped and the ice cream isn't frozen too hard. Once the meal is cooked, it's time to release your mind and relax!

straight-talk turkey

serves 10 to 12 (with leftovers)

No brining or babysitting is needed for this recipe—just a good bird, started from room temperature, cooked in a calibrated oven (meaning you know the *exact* inside temperature—ask at the hardware store for the $4 oven thermometer that hooks onto a rack) for the amount of time needed for your size bird (see below), and finished when an instant-read thermometer reaches 165°F. This turkey can be cooked stuffed with Fig and Pancetta Stuffing or Basic Bread Stuffing (page 220). Or it does not have to be stuffed at all.

One whole turkey, patted dry

2 tablespoons coarse salt

1 teaspoon freshly ground black pepper

6 cups Fig and Pancetta Stuffing or Basic Bread Stuffing (page 220), optional

IF UNSTUFFED

1 orange, halved

1 lemon, halved

1 small yellow onion, quartered

1 head garlic, halved

6 sprigs fresh thyme

2 sprigs fresh sage

1 tablespoon olive oil

4 cups chicken broth or water, warmed

½ cup milk

2 tablespoons all-purpose flour

1 Preheat the oven to 425°F with the rack in the lower third of the oven. Season the cavity of the turkey with 1 tablespoon of the salt and ½ teaspoon of the pepper. Stuff the cavity with stuffing or the orange, lemon, onion, garlic, and herbs. Tie the legs with twine and transfer the turkey to a rack set inside a roasting pan. Rub the skin with the oil and season with the remaining 1 tablespoon salt and ½ teaspoon pepper.

2 Pour 2 cups of the broth into the roasting pan and transfer to the oven. Roast the turkey for 30 minutes, then reduce the oven temperature to 350°F. After the first hour of roasting, baste the turkey every 30 minutes. (Tent the turkey with foil if the skin becomes a deep golden brown before the turkey is cooked.) Roast until a meat thermometer inserted into the thigh joint registers 160°F. (If roasting a 12-pound bird, check the temperature after 1½ hours. A 14-pounder should take 2½ to 3 hours; a 20-pounder 4½ to 5. A stuffed bird will be on the longer side.) Remove the turkey from the oven and transfer to a carving board. Let the turkey rest for at least 20 minutes.

3 Meanwhile, place the roasting pan on the stovetop over medium-high heat. Add the remaining broth to the pan drippings and bring to a simmer. Combine the milk and flour in a jar with a tight-fitting lid and shake vigorously to combine. Whisk the milk mixture into the gravy and simmer, whisking continuously, until the gravy thickens slightly, about 2 minutes.

4 Carve the turkey and serve with gravy.

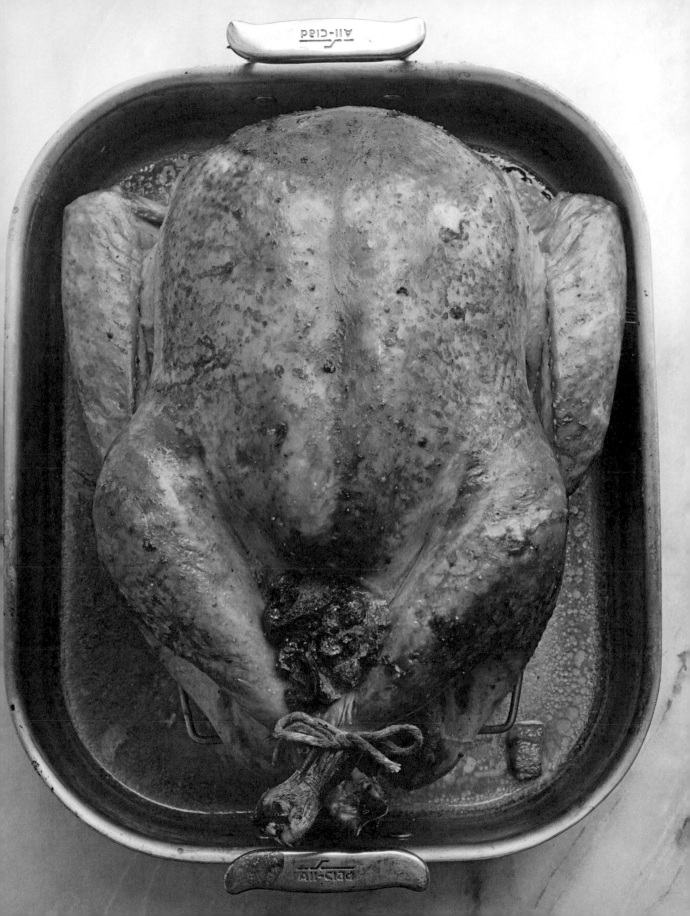

thanksgiving leftover pie

serves 6 to 8

Otherwise known as Danksgiving Leftover Pie (from the slang word "dank," which my sons use to describe all things awe-inspiring), this idea came from my savory pie–loving firstborn son on the day after Thanksgiving. There is only enough for one pie, and one slice per person—a teaser that leaves you longing to make it again the next year. And yes, it even one-ups the deliciousness of a leftover sandwich.

4 tablespoons (½ stick) unsalted butter

2 carrots, chopped

2 celery stalks, chopped

1 small onion, chopped

¼ cup all-purpose flour, or 2 tablespoons cornstarch

Coarse salt and freshly ground black pepper

2 cups Turkey Broth (see opposite) or chicken broth

3 to 4 cups shredded leftover cooked turkey

1 recipe Cream Cheese Pastry Dough (page 91)

Leftover stuffing

Leftover mashed potatoes

Leftover vegetables

Leftover gravy

1 large egg yolk, beaten with a little milk or cream

Leftover cranberry sauce

1 Melt the butter in a large skillet over medium heat. Add the carrots, celery, and onions and sauté to soften, about 2 minutes. Sprinkle the flour over the vegetables and cook, stirring, for 2 minutes. Whisk in the stock and cook until slightly thickened, 3 to 4 minutes. Remove from the heat, fold in the turkey meat, and set aside to cool.

2 Roll out 1 disc of dough and place it in a 9-inch pie plate. Trim the dough so it's flush with the edge of the dish. Spread a layer of stuffing over the bottom of the dough. Pile on the turkey mixture and smooth to a dome shape. Spread the mashed potatoes on top. Distribute any leftover vegetables over the potatoes. Poke three or four holes in the filling mixture and spoon some gravy into the holes.

3 Roll out the remaining dough and place it on top of the filled pie. Trim it so it drapes about ½ inch over the lower crust. Slightly lift up the bottom edge of the lower crust and tuck the top crust of dough underneath it. Press the dough with your fingertips or a fork to seal. Chill the pie in the refrigerator for 15 minutes to firm the dough.

4 Preheat the oven to 400°F. Brush the egg wash over the dough and make four slits on the top. Place the pie on a baking sheet and bake for 15 minutes, then reduce the heat to 375°F. Bake for 45 to 55 minutes more (check the pie after 45 minutes). The top should be golden brown and the bottom a light golden brown. Remove the pie from the oven and transfer it to a cooling rack. Let it rest for at least 30 minutes and up to 1 hour (the longer the pie rests, the easier it will be to slice). Cut into pieces. Serve with warm gravy on one side and a dollop of cool leftover cranberry sauce on the other.

HOW TO MAKE TURKEY BROTH

To make turkey stock from the picked-over carcass, put it in a large pot and
add water to cover the bones. Throw in an onion and bring to a boil. Simmer for
about 45 minutes (not too long because spent bones have little flavor). Strain the
broth through a cheesecloth-lined sieve (you can use a clean dishcloth instead
of cheesecloth). Return the strained broth to the pot and boil until reduced by a
quarter to concentrate the flavor. Season with salt at the end.

CHRISTMAS: THE MEAL, THE MENU, THE MEAT

Our family's Christmas meal has been the same for twenty-seven years. It is inspired by memories from my grandparents' home— and grew from a determination to one day cook his rib roast myself.

In my grandfather's house, it didn't matter if you wanted medium or well-done meat—you had to eat it rare because that's how it was "supposed" to be eaten: practically walking off the plate. I quickly discovered the "first slice." The outside slice was not only well cooked but was coated in the seasoning, too. Now that I cook the roast myself, I know how to make the inside blood red, with plenty of gradating degrees of doneness as you move to either end.

This meal is one of the big family Christmas gifts—when you think of it that way, you won't mind investing in the meat, which is not cheap.

THE MENU

Standing Rib Roast and Gravy (page 215)

Hedgehog Potatoes (see opposite)

Yorkshire Pudding (page 216)

Peas, Pearl Onions, and Mint (page 224)

Dessert of the Year (last year's was store-bought Fortnum and Mason Christmas Plum Pudding with hard sauce)

Let's look at every element:

Gravy: since the whole plate will likely be covered in gravy, I take the time to properly prepare for it. When shopping for the holidays, get a bunch of beef bones from the butcher and use them to make broth (see opposite).

Meat: let your meat sit out for 2 hours to come to room temperature. Season it an hour before you plan to roast it. A four-rib roast will cook in about 2 hours, which gives you time to get everything else cooked and organized (since all ovens are different, cooking time will vary). Make sure you have at least one instant-read thermometer on hand (I use two—one to corroborate the findings of the first). Pay close attention during the last half hour, which is when the meat starts to cook fast. You must pull it from the oven when the thermometer reads between 125 and 130°F; once out of the oven, the residual heat will continue to cook the meat (you want to end up at 135°F). Pour about ¼ inch of water into the pan before roasting and continue to keep an eye on that, too. The juices and fat will start flowing after the first hour, but until that happens you don't want a scorched-pan smell to mess up your baby.

Hedgehog potatoes: peel the potatoes and let sit in salted cold water. Cook them in advance, then let cool slightly and score from end to end with the tines of a fork. Scatter the potatoes around the roast for the last hour of cooking. They will get golden brown and crispy—especially around all those vertical indentations. Yum.

Meanwhile, be prepared for the individual Yorkies: as soon as the meat comes out of the oven, transfer it to your cutting board and tent it with foil to rest for at least 30 minutes. Pour the beef fat into a Pyrex pitcher and set the pan aside for making the gravy.

Yorkshire pudding: when the meat comes out of the oven, have your popover or muffin tins ready and put them in the oven to heat up.

Now work fast! Finish the gravy, complete the peas, get everything at the table or buffet, and start slicing the meat. Those puffed-up pinnacles of Yorkshire pudding perfection should be the last thing you pull from the oven as you sit down.

Yes, it's a bit of a dance at the end, but if everything is prepped and ready to go, timers are set, and thermometers are used, you'll make the easiest yet grandest feast there is to eat.

beef broth

Place beef bones in a roasting pan and roast at 375°F until golden brown, about 45 minutes. Then put them (along with any beefy juices) in a pot, throw in some carrot, celery, onion, parsley, garlic, and peppercorns. Cover with water, bring to a boil, skim off the scum, and let the pot simmer, partially covered, for up to 2 hours (the full 2 hours is optimal). Strain the liquid, return it to the pot, and simmer until it reduces to about a quart. Chill and skim the fat. You now have an amazing broth with which to make your gravy. It will keep for 2 days in the fridge and 6 to 8 weeks in the freezer.

standing rib roast

serves 10 to 12

The hardest part of this recipe is the price of the meat. Do not be surprised if it runs you $15 to $20 a pound—and you'll need 9 or 10 pounds of it. Since you've invested so much, pay attention as it cooks (see page 212). Since all ovens are different, times will vary. The ribs form their own rack, so all that's needed is a nice sturdy roasting pan or a large pan with 2-inch-tall sides.
I always serve this with prepared horseradish on the table.

One 4- to 6-rib beef roast, trimmed, at room temperature (it will take at least an hour out of the refrigerator)

2 tablespoons dry or Dijon mustard

2 tablespoons sugar

2 teaspoons coarse salt

1 teaspoon freshly ground black pepper

Extra-virgin olive oil

1 Preheat the oven to 450°F with the rack in the lower third of the oven. Lightly score the fat on top of the meat in a diamond pattern. Place in a roasting pan, rib side down. Combine the mustard, sugar, salt, and pepper and rub the mixture all over the meat. If need be, mix another batch of the dry rub in order to fully coat the meat. Drizzle a little oil over the top of the meat and pour enough water into the bottom of the pan to reach a depth of ¼ inch (this prevents smoking).

2 Place the roast in the oven. After 15 minutes, reduce the heat to 375°F and continue to roast, basting frequently, until an instant-read thermometer registers between 125 and 130°F for medium-rare, about 1 hour and 45 minutes. Start checking the temperature of the meat after 1 hour; the meat will cook quickly during the last half hour. Total cooking time is about 2 hours for a 5-rib roast.

3 Transfer the roast to a cutting board, tented loosely with foil, for at least 20 minutes (the internal temperature should rise to 135°F). Reserve the pan juices for gravy, and the fat for Yorkshire pudding. Use a very sharp knife to carve the meat.

KILLER GRAVY

Place the roasting pan across two burners over medium heat (reserving any fat you might need from the pan for Yorkshire pudding). Combine ½ cup beef broth (page 213) and ¼ cup all-purpose flour in a lidded jar and shake until well combined. Slowly whisk the flour mixture into the pan, scraping up the browned bits, and cook until thick and bubbling, about 2 minutes. Slowly add the remaining stock (a little less than 1 quart) to the pan, whisk to combine, and simmer until slightly thickened, about 5 minutes. Strain if too lumpy.

yorkshire pudding

makes 12

In my house, it *might* still be Christmas without the beef, but the holiday would effectively be called off without the Yorkshire pudding. Every year, regardless of the guest count, I double the batter (which can be made several hours in advance) and get ready to stick a second batch in the oven just as we sit down to dinner with the first batch! If you don't use it up, refrigerate it overnight, and make a batch in the morning for a fresh-baked addition to leftovers. Muffin tins will work just fine, but for the deepest, largest puffed beauties, get a popover pan. And the secret to the highest, puffiest popovers is to have the batter at room temperature and to preheat the greased pan so that when the batter hits, the rise begins immediately (though you won't see it right away).

4 large eggs, at room temperature

3¼ cups whole milk

2 cups all-purpose flour

1½ teaspoons coarse salt

¼ teaspoon freshly ground black pepper

4 tablespoons pan drippings, reserved from the beef roast (see page 215)

1 Preheat the oven to 400°F. Place foil or a sheet pan below the rack you're using for the Yorkies to catch any overflow. Place the eggs, milk, flour, salt, and pepper in a blender and blend on high until the mixture is combined and resembles heavy cream. (This can be done several hours in advance.)

2 Pour 1 teaspoon pan drippings into each popover cup (half that amount if using a muffin tin). Heat in the oven for 2 minutes.

3 Quickly and carefully pour the batter into the cups, filling each about halfway. Put directly in the oven and do not open the door; keep the light on to watch what's going on in there! Bake until puffed and golden brown, about 30 minutes (the Yorkies will puff to the highest height, but not until the last 10 minutes of cooking time). Serve immediately.

ONE BIG PUDDING

This batter will also bake beautifully in one 9-by-13-inch pan. Preheat the oven to 400°F, add a couple of tablespoons of beef fat to the pan, and pour in the batter. Bake as directed above.

stuffed capon

serves 6 to 8

A capon is a castrated rooster that has been fattened up for eating and yields the most chickeny chicken flavor ever—even edging a little closer to the flavor of its gamey cousins pheasant and quail. It's a special alternative to turkey for a holiday meal. I like to make one for New Year's dinner. Save the carcass to make a killer soup (following the method described on page 211).

1 tablespoon butter or olive oil

One 7- to 8-pound capon

Coarse salt and freshly ground black pepper

2 cups Fig and Pancetta Stuffing or Basic Bread Stuffing (page 220)

3 tablespoons cornstarch, or ¼ cup all-purpose flour

2 cups chicken broth, homemade (opposite) or store-bought

1 Preheat the oven to 450°F with the rack in the lower third of the oven. Rub the butter or oil all over the capon and generously season, including inside the cavity, with salt and pepper. Loosely spoon the stuffing inside the bird. The legs can be tied together with twine, but I prefer to let them splay open so as much skin and stuffing surface as possible crisps up and turns golden brown. (For any remaining stuffing, see page 220 for instructions on how to bake separately.)

2 Place the bird, breast side down, on an oiled rack in a large roasting pan. Pour 2 cups water into the pan to prevent smoking. Check periodically to ensure the pan is not dry.

WORTH KNOWING

HOW TO GET SUPER-CRISPY SKIN

Once the bird is cleaned, pour boiling water over the skin, which will firm and tighten it. Pat dry. Additionally, you can place the bird, uncovered, on a rack and refrigerate it overnight—this will further dry out the skin, a necessity for crispiness. Remove the chicken from the refrigerator at least 30 minutes and up to 2 hours before cooking.

3 After 20 minutes, reduce the oven temperature to 375°F. Turn the bird over, breast side up, and continue to cook until a meat thermometer registers about 160°F, 1½ to 2 hours. The internal temperature of the bird accelerates rapidly, so pay close attention after 1 hour of roasting and check every 15 minutes. The temperature should be checked in a couple of places, both between the leg and thigh joint and in the thickest part of the breast. Once the bird is out of the oven, there will be some carryover cooking that will increase the temperature a little bit.

4 Remove the capon from the oven and transfer to a carving board. Lightly tent with foil and let rest for 20 minutes before carving and serving. (This is important to keep the bird juicy.)

5 Place the roasting pan on the stovetop over medium-high heat. If the pan fits over two burners, turn them both on. Whisk in the cornstarch and cook for 2 minutes. Slowly pour in the broth, whisking to break up any lumps and fully combine the juices, thickener, and liquid. Simmer until slightly thickened, adding more broth, if needed, to reach your desired consistency. Season with salt and pepper, if needed.

roast chicken broth

Browning the chicken parts before boiling creates a deep, rich flavor—a great complement to the caramelization of roasted meat. Season 2 pounds of the chicken parts with salt and pepper. Brown in butter in a roasting pan over two burners, along with a chopped onion, 2 celery stalks, and 2 carrots. Add 10 cups of water and simmer for 1 hour. Strain and reduce to 4 cups.

fig and pancetta stuffing (or dressing)

makes 1½ quarts

The contrast between the sweet figs and salty pancetta here provides deep, rich overall flavor. This is an excellent stuffing for roast turkey, like Straight-Talk Turkey (page 208), Stuffed Capon (page 218), and regular chicken, too.

2 tablespoons unsalted butter, plus more for the baking dish

1 small yellow onion, chopped

6 ounces pancetta, chopped into ¼-inch pieces

1 teaspoon coarse salt

1½ cups chicken broth

8 ounces black Mission figs, coarsely chopped

Finely grated zest and juice of 1 orange

2 tablespoons orange liqueur, such as triple sec, or white wine (optional)

1 tablespoon finely chopped fresh sage

12 slices whole wheat bread, torn or cubed and dried (6 to 8 cups)

2 large eggs, lightly beaten (use if cooking the stuffing outside the bird in a baking dish)

1 Melt the butter in a medium pan over medium-high heat. Add the onions, pancetta, and salt and cook, stirring occasionally, until the pancetta begins to render its fat, the onions become translucent with lightly caramelized edges, and a cheesy scent develops, 8 to 9 minutes. Add the broth and figs and bring to a boil, scraping the browned bits from the bottom of the pan. Remove from the heat and let stand for 10 minutes to plump the figs, stirring occasionally.

2 Add the orange zest and juice, liqueur (if using), and sage to the pan and stir to combine. Pour the contents of the saucepan over the bread pieces in a large bowl and stir until well combined. If using to stuff a bird, cool the stuffing and follow the cooking instructions for that recipe. If using as a dressing (or if you have extra after stuffing your bird), stir in the beaten eggs and transfer the mixture to a buttered 2½-quart baking dish. Cover with foil and bake at 350°F for 30 minutes. Remove the foil and continue baking until the top is golden brown and crispy, 10 to 15 minutes more.

BASIC BREAD STUFFING

Sauté a chopped onion and a couple of sliced celery stalks in butter and deglaze with a glug of white wine, then throw in a small handful of chopped sage, and 4 cups dry bread cubes made from any favorite or leftover bread. (If starting with a fresh loaf, cube it and dry it at 200°F for 1 hour.) Dampen the bread mixture with 1 cup or more chicken broth, season with salt and pepper, and let cool. Now you're good to stuff the bird!

middle eastern stuffed lamb roll

serves 6 to 8

Sometimes you just want to try something new. Spring stirs the experimenter in me, and this leg of lamb was born when a bout of recipe wanderlust coincided with an Easter holiday. I dug deeper into the wonderful flavors of the eastern Mediterranean, and detoured from my standard bone-in, lemon-garlic-rosemary leg of lamb recipe. The lamb here—boned and butterflied—is stuffed with a spiced, fragrant rice mixture that perfumes and infuses the roasted meat. For this, you'll need at least 3 feet of butcher's twine or string.

1 tablespoon extra-virgin olive oil, plus more for rubbing on the lamb

1 small onion, chopped

2 garlic cloves, minced

1 tablespoon ground coriander or garam masala

1 teaspoon ground cinnamon

1 teaspoon ground cumin

2 cups basmati rice, rinsed and drained

½ cup dried red cherries

3 cups chicken broth

Pinch of saffron (optional)

1½ teaspoons coarse salt, plus more as needed

½ cup toasted salted pistachios or sliced almonds, coarsely chopped

One 4- to 5-pound boneless leg of lamb, butterflied and trimmed of excess fat, at room temperature

Freshly ground black pepper

2 tablespoons pomegranate molasses or honey

1 Heat a medium pot over medium heat. Swirl in the oil. When it shimmers, add the onions and garlic and cook until translucent, about 3 minutes. Add the coriander, cinnamon, and cumin and toast for 2 minutes. Add the rice and stir to cook and coat with the spices, about 2 minutes. Add the cherries.

2 Stir in the broth, saffron (if using), and salt. Raise the heat to high and bring to a full rolling boil. Cover, reduce the heat to low, and simmer until all the liquid has absorbed, about 20 minutes. Spread the rice mixture on a buking sheet and stir in the pistachios. Let cool.

3 Preheat the oven to 425°F. Open up the lamb and lay it flat on a parchment paper–lined surface. Generously season with salt and pepper. Spread 1 to 2 cups of the rice stuffing over the surface of the lamb (reserve the remaining rice to serve as a side dish). Starting at the most narrow end (and using the parchment to lift and assist in rolling), roll the lamb, tucking the stuffing in as you turn it. Secure the roll with a rubber band at each end.

4 With butcher's twine or string, tie the lamb from side to side to secure the meat in a roll. Cut off and discard the rubber bands. Place the meat on a rack inside a roasting pan. Rub the meat with oil and season with

salt and pepper. Add 2 cups water to the roasting pan. (Add more water as needed to keep the bottom of the pan from scorching and burning.)

5 Roast for 15 minutes, then reduce the heat to 350°F and roast until an instant-read thermometer inserted into the thickest part registers 135°F, about 1½ hours more (start checking the temperature after 1 hour).

6 Preheat the broiler. Brush the lamb with the pomegranate molasses and broil, a couple of inches away from the flame, until the top is lightly caramelized, 2 to 3 minutes. (The internal temperature will continue to rise as the meat broils; it should reach 140 to 145°F for medium-rare). Transfer the lamb to a cutting board, tent with foil, and let it rest for 15 to 20 minutes. Slice and serve.

BALANCING ACT

I serve my favorite sides with this lamb: Tabbouleh Salad (from *Mad Hungry: Feeding Men & Boys*), Spinach Phyllo Pie (from *Mad Hungry Cravings*), and steamed asparagus. If you are strategizing a large holiday meal with the lamb as your centerpiece, here are a couple of tips: The stuffing can be made in advance, cooled, and refrigerated for a couple of days. The spinach pie can be made and frozen, uncooked, far ahead, and slipped right from the freezer into the oven while the lamb is resting. The tabbouleh can be made up to a day ahead, since its flavors deepen with time. Greek Yogurt Cake (from *Mad Hungry Cravings*) is an awesome dessert for this meal.

SEVEN SIMPLE SIDES

Uncomplicated options—these are the secret to maintaining your cooking composure while rounding out a holiday main course with vibrant vegetable side dishes. When everything is prepped in advance—and by this I mean washed, cut, thawed, or chopped—they can cook in just that sliver of time when the beef, turkey, capon, or lamb is resting out of the oven. With fresh, well-chosen produce you won't need any more than a few added ingredients to create a complete, delicious, and satisfying dish like the ones here.

Peas, pearl onions, and mint: thaw frozen pearl onions (or chop regular ones). Sauté the onions in olive oil, add thawed frozen peas, toss around to heat through (add an optional handful of baby spinach or butter lettuce to wilt), and fold in fresh mint leaves. Season to taste.

Green beans and toasted almonds: place trimmed beans in a pan with a knob of butter and a cup of water. Simmer until the water has evaporated and the beans are just tender and are caramelizing in the butter. Add a handful of toasted almonds. Season to taste.

Carrots, shallots, and vinegar: slice or chop carrots into bite-size pieces and place in a saucepan with ½ cup water, some minced shallots, a glug of olive oil, and salt. Simmer until the water has evaporated. Sprinkle with a large pinch of sugar, pour in a good slug of red wine vinegar, and stir until the liquid turns into a glaze and the carrots are tender. Toss with fresh tarragon or basil, if desired.

Brussels sprouts, red onion, and lemon: trim and halve the Brussels sprouts lengthwise (quarter them if they are very large). Place on a baking sheet with a small chopped red onion and a lemon that has been quartered and thinly sliced. Add olive oil, salt, and pepper and toss to coat. Roast at 400°F for 25 minutes. Replace the lemon with chopped bacon, if desired.

Sweet potatoes, garlic, and rosemary: halve small sweet potatoes or coarsely chop peeled large ones. Place on a baking sheet with several smashed and whole peeled garlic cloves. Add olive oil, salt, and several sprigs of fresh rosemary and toss to coat. Roast at 400°F for 30 minutes.

Red cabbage, dill, and orange: core and shred the cabbage. Sauté it in olive oil or butter in a large skillet. Add minced garlic and a glug of water. Cook until just tender and the liquid has evaporated. Squeeze in the juice from half an orange and add a handful of chopped fresh dill. Season to taste.

Sliced mushrooms, black pepper, and parsley: melt butter in a large skillet; add the mushrooms and lots of ground black pepper. Cook, stirring until all the liquid has been released and evaporated and mushrooms begin to brown. Season with salt and add a handful of chopped fresh parsley.

SPEED-SCRATCH SWEETS

OPPOSITE: Sticky Chocolate Spoonfuls (page 249)

EASY-DOES-IT DESSERTS

When you routinely get breakfast, lunch, and dinner on the table, it's understandable that you might be inclined to "close the kitchen" as soon as the last dinner plate is scraped. But if your house is like mine—a mad hungry one—there is always an insatiable mouth in the group that pipes up with an "Is there anything sweet to eat?" (By the way, it's perfectly admissible if yours is the mouth asking this.)

Sometimes a nice piece of fresh fruit will do the trick. For the other 364 nights of the year, I recommend a well-stocked pantry: an assortment of packaged goods that will get you halfway to something sweet and delicious in record time. A pint of ice cream, a sleeve of cookies, a spoonful of peanut butter— these are some of the things that enable you to rustle up a dessert while still managing the mealtime mountains that are scaled several times each day. Beyond the usual baking staples of sugar, baking powder, cocoa, vanilla extract, and spices, here are some simple sweets to keep on hand:

PANTRY

lemon curd • Nutella • canned peaches • instant espresso powder • cocoa powder • sweetened condensed milk • semisweet chocolate bar • candied ginger • Medjool dates • amaretti cookies • sweetened whole-meal English biscuits, such as McVitie's Digestives • unsweetened coconut flakes • honey • rum • gelatin

FREEZER

frozen berries • packaged puff pastry • wonton skins • dried fruit, such as cranberries, cherries, apricots, currants, and raisins • variety of nuts

SALTY, SWEET, AND SPICY

candied cashews

makes 1 pint

Candied nuts are a really satisfying snack to serve with chocolate and fresh or dried fruit for a quick dessert. You can also whip up a batch for cocktail hour or use them as gifts.

1 teaspoon ground cinnamon

1 teaspoon coarse salt

¾ teaspoon ground coriander

¼ teaspoon ground allspice

⅛ teaspoon cayenne

2 cups roasted cashews

½ cup sugar

¼ cup water

1 In a small bowl, combine the cinnamon, salt, coriander, allspice, and cayenne. Combine the cashews, sugar, and water in a large skillet and bring to a boil over high heat. Lower the heat and simmer, stirring frequently, until the water has evaporated and the sugar crystallizes around the nuts, about 5 minutes.

2 Stir the spice mixture into the nuts and continue cooking, stirring continuously, until the sugar begins to melt and caramelize, 1 to 2 minutes. Transfer the nuts to a parchment paper–lined baking sheet, cool to room temperature, and separate before serving.

SUNDAE SAMPLE

coffee cookie parfait

serves 2

Making dessert can be daunting, especially if you aren't a natural baker. Don't be deterred. Parfaits are the perfect vehicle for the best cheater-dessert. By layering everyday ingredients together in clear glasses, you create something that appears way more fancy than it really is.

½ cup crushed amaretti cookies, plus 2 whole cookies for serving

2 scoops coffee ice cream

2 scoops vanilla ice cream

2 spoonfuls Candied Cashews (above; optional)

Divide a third of the crushed amaretti cookies between two parfait glasses. Place a scoop of coffee ice cream in each glass and sprinkle another third of crushed cookies into the glasses. Top each glass with a scoop of vanilla ice cream and the remaining crushed cookies. Garnish each parfait with a whole cookie and a spoonful of cashews, if you wish.

peach kuchen

makes 18 pieces

A kuchen recipe often refers to a German cake. This one is more like the happy baby of a cake and a pie. The peaches are suspended in a cinnamon custard, which sets up on top of a loose crust. It's the first dessert I learned from the first chef I worked with, and it's a great addition to any non-baker's arsenal of desserts because it's so *easy* to make successfully. If you can make scrambled eggs, you can swing this.

2 cups all-purpose flour

½ cup (1 stick) salted butter

½ cup plus 2 teaspoons sugar

¼ teaspoon coarse salt

1 teaspoon baking powder

6 freestone peaches, peeled and halved, or two 29-ounce cans peaches packed in juice, drained

1 tablespoon ground cinnamon

1 cup heavy cream

2 large egg yolks

1 Preheat the oven to 400°F. Place the flour, butter, 2 teaspoons of the sugar, the salt, and baking powder in a 9-by-13-inch baking dish. Cut the ingredients together until the mixture resembles cornmeal. With your hands, press the mixture onto the bottom and up the sides of the pan to cover it evenly.

2 Arrange the peaches, cut side down, evenly over the crust. In a small bowl, combine the remaining ½ cup sugar and the cinnamon and sprinkle it over the peaches. Bake until the crust begins to turn golden and the sugar is bubbling, about 10 minutes.

3 Meanwhile, whisk together the heavy cream and egg yolks in a medium bowl. Remove the kuchen from the oven and pour the cream mixture over the peaches. Lower the oven temperature to 350°F, return the kuchen to the oven, and bake until the custard is set, 20 to 30 minutes. Allow the kuchen to cool slightly, then cut and serve warm.

ABOUT CANNED PEACHES

Let's get one thing straight: some processed fruits are actually tastier and more nutritious than poorly handled, out-of-season fresh fruit. When the pantry is stocked with a good collection of usable alternatives, your cooking and baking options open wide, no matter what time of year it is. In my fantasy life, I pickle, can, and jam everything myself, but . . . yeah, that's not going to happen. When I buy canned fruit, I read labels, avoid sugary packing syrups, and buy organic whenever possible. Peaches packed in juice—not syrup— are a poster child for canned fruit.

upside-down apple tart

serves 6

Classically called a tarte tatin, the *ne plus ultra* of French desserts, this version is a no-fail, easy-to-pull-off yet impressive *and* delicious dessert. To serve, top with a scoop of vanilla ice cream or whipped cream.

3½ pounds apples, such as Gala

Juice of 1 lemon

6 tablespoons (¾ stick) unsalted butter, at room temperature

¾ cup sugar

½ teaspoon coarse salt

1 sheet puff pastry, thawed according to package instructions

All-purpose flour, for dusting

½ teaspoon ground cinnamon

1 Preheat the oven to 425°F. Peel, core, and quarter the apples lengthwise. As each one is peeled, toss with the lemon juice to prevent browning.

2 Spread 5 tablespoons of the butter evenly over the bottom and up the sides of a 10-inch cast-iron or other oven-safe skillet. Sprinkle ½ cup of the sugar and the salt evenly over the bottom of the skillet. Arrange the apple slices around the edge of the pan in circles, working toward the center of the skillet.

3 Place the skillet over medium heat and cook, undisturbed, for 18 minutes. Transfer the pan to the oven and bake until the apples have softened and shrunken slightly, about 20 minutes.

4 Meanwhile, roll out the puff pastry on a lightly floured surface to an 11-inch square. Using a plate as a guide, cut out a 10-inch circle and transfer it to a parchment paper–lined baking sheet. Chill until needed.

5 When the apples are ready, melt the remaining 1 tablespoon butter and brush it over the pastry. Combine the remaining ¼ cup sugar and the cinnamon in a small bowl and sprinkle it over the pastry. Slide the pastry, cinnamon side down, over the apples. Return the skillet to the oven and bake until the pastry is golden and brown, about 20 minutes.

6 Cool on a wire rack for 10 minutes and then slide a knife around the edge of the pastry to loosen and invert onto a serving plate. Cut into wedges to serve.

toasted angel food and lemon curd with berries and cream

serves 6

This dessert only looks like you've done a lot of work. It is actually one of those entirely composed desserts, assembled (not made!) from store-bought ingredients.

3 tablespoons unsalted butter

6 slices store-bought angel food cake

¾ cup store-bought lemon curd

1½ cups heavy cream

1 tablespoon sugar

1½ cups berries

1 Melt the butter in a large nonstick pan over medium-high heat. Toast the angel food cake slices in the butter, flipping once, until golden brown on both sides, 2 to 3 minutes total. Transfer to six dessert plates.

2 Spoon the lemon curd evenly over the cake slices. Whip together the cream and sugar until soft peaks form. Dollop the whipped cream on or next to the cake slices. Garnish with berries and serve.

{

WAYS WITH LEMON CURD

Here are a few more uses for lemon curd (I like Wilkens & Sons Ltd.):

Dollop it over scoops of vanilla ice cream. ★ **Stir it** into plain yogurt. ★ **Spread it** over French toast. ★ **Fold it** into whipped cream and top with crumbled cookies. ★ **Fill** a blind-baked pastry shell with it. ★ **Sandwich it** between oatmeal cookies. ★ **Slather it** over blueberry pancakes.

}

three melon salad

serves 8

There are times when you crave sugary desserts like a crisp or crumble, and times when you want refreshingly fruity ones. Different melons, such as orange cantaloupe, pink watermelon, or green honeydew, present a vibrant array of colors and tones, and when teamed with fresh herbs, they combine for a satisfying nonfat salad or dessert. Sometimes, I'll put a different color of melon in its own clear bowl and use a different herb for each one. Fresh lemon verbena, mint, cilantro, and basil would complement any of the melons.

½ cantaloupe

½ green melon, such as honeydew or Santa Claus

½ small seedless watermelon

¼ cup loosely packed fresh mint leaves

Juice of 1 lime

1 Scrape out the seeds from the melon halves, then cut the melon halves into ½-inch slices and cube each one, cutting off the peels as you work. You will have about 2 cups cantaloupe, 2½ cups honeydew, and 3½ cups watermelon.

2 Place the fruit in a large serving bowl. Tear the mint leaves over the melon salad and pour the lime juice over all. Toss gently to mix.

WORTH KNOWING

HOW TO CHOOSE A MELON

When you're faced with that sometimes daunting task of choosing a melon, there are a few things you can do to ensure that you get a good one.

First, lift up the melon. It should be heavy for its size, which means it's suitably juicy.

Knock the outside of several fruits. A high-pitched sound indicates an unripe fruit, while a low-pitched one can be overripe. Choose something in the middle.

Smell it. Regardless of what variety you're choosing, it should smell slightly sweet and reminiscent of how the flesh tastes. If it has no scent, it'll have no flavor.

strawberry vanilla ice cream cake

serves 8

I love this cake. Sweetened balsamic vinegar blends beautifully with strawberries for a slightly tangy yet still sweet undercurrent to the fragrant berries. Blended together and formed into a loaf cake, it's an effortless transformation of a few ingredients into something unexpected.

2 pints strawberries, washed and hulled

¼ cup sugar

1½ tablespoons balsamic vinegar

One 28-ounce carton vanilla ice cream

Vanilla cookies, for serving

1 Place the strawberries, sugar, and vinegar in a food processor or blender and purée until very smooth.

2 Line an 8-inch square glass baking dish with plastic wrap. Pour in the strawberry mixture and freeze until barely firm, about 2 hours. Meanwhile, remove the ice cream from the freezer to soften up.

3 Spread the softened ice cream evenly over the firm purée. Freeze until both are firm, at least 2 hours. To serve, pull on the plastic wrap to turn the "cake" onto a platter. Flip, so that the strawberries are on the bottom, and cut into squares. Serve each square with a vanilla cookie.

mocha panna cotta

serves 8

Make this dessert when you want to serve something special that can be done completely in advance, with no last-minute fussing.

2 envelopes gelatin (16 ounces)

6 tablespoons cold water

2 cups heavy cream

2 cups whole milk

¼ cup sugar

2 tablespoons instant espresso powder

Pinch of coarse salt

6 ounces semisweet chocolate, chopped (about ½ cup), plus more for serving

1 Sprinkle the gelatin over the cold water in a small bowl. Let stand to soften, 5 to 8 minutes. Meanwhile, whisk together the cream and milk in a saucepan and heat over medium heat until just hot to the touch. Stir in the sugar, espresso powder, and salt until they have dissolved.

2 Pour the hot milk mixture over the chopped chocolate in a large bowl and stir until melted and incorporated. Whisk 1 cup of the warm chocolate mixture into the dissolved gelatin to combine and melt the gelatin. Return the gelatin mixture to the bowl with the chocolate mixture and whisk to fully combine.

3 Divide the mixture among eight 8-ounce ramekins, filling each one halfway. Refrigerate for at least 3 hours and up to overnight. To serve, dip the bottoms of the ramekins in hot water for a few seconds and run a small knife around the edges to release the custard. Turn out onto a plate and garnish with chopped chocolate.

vanilla cup custards

serves 6

There is something universally appealing about a sweet creamy custard. That gentle vanilla flavor is delicious eaten plain for a simple dessert—or you can dress it up with shaved chocolate, fresh berries, or cookies on the side. Don't toss those egg whites—they can be frozen for future use!

1 cup heavy cream

1 cup whole milk

1 vanilla bean, split and seeds scraped, or 1 teaspoon pure vanilla extract

¼ teaspoon coarse salt

6 large egg yolks

⅓ cup sugar

Freshly grated nutmeg, for serving

1 Preheat the oven to 325°F. Put a kettle of water on the stove to boil. Bring the cream, milk, vanilla bean seeds and pod (or extract), and salt to a simmer in a small saucepan over medium heat. If using a vanilla bean, simmer for about 10 minutes to infuse the flavors and strain into a measuring cup. Otherwise, just heat through.

2 Whisk the egg yolks with the sugar in a medium bowl until fully incorporated. Slowly pour the cream mixture into the yolks, whisking continuously. Transfer this custard to a large measuring pitcher to make it easy to pour.

3 Place six 4- or 6-ounce ramekins inside a roasting pan. Divide the custard evenly among them. Carefully pour enough boiling water into the roasting pan to come halfway up the sides of the ramekins. Transfer the roasting pan to the oven and bake until the custards are just set, 25 to 30 minutes. Remove the ramekins from the oven and roasting pan and let the custards cool. Refrigerate for at least 2 hours and up to overnight until chilled completely. Sprinkle freshly grated nutmeg over the custards just before serving.

WORTH KNOWING

HOW TO TEMPER EGGS

When you are making an egg-rich custard—and understandably desire a smoothly gelled pudding rather than something resembling scrambled eggs—you must slowly and gently add the hot liquid to the beaten eggs. If you dump the hot mixture in too quickly, lumps will form. Whisking vigorously, you want to slowly and gradually incorporate the hot milk mixture, allowing the eggs time to acclimate to the warm temperature, thereby maintaining a silky smoothness.

DON'T FORGET TO BUY BANANAS

It's inexpensive. It comes in its own wrapper. It doesn't require assiduous rinsing before eating. And it is the cheeriest shade of yellow. There's nothing easier to eat on the go than a banana, the original portable fast food. But this wonder food also produces a luscious sweet flavor when cooked into bread, layered into an ice cream sundae, or blended in a milk shake. Every time you go to the grocery store, buy a couple or a bunch. Eat or use them according to their color, as described below.

Snack on bananas at their peak ripeness, when they're nice and yellow and devoid of brown dents. Or toss a couple into the dying embers of a barbecue fire to cook while you eat dinner, slice open the charred skin, and add a scoop of vanilla ice cream. No easier dessert exists.

Just slightly riper bananas—those in the brown freckles stage—make fruit smoothies better by bringing sweetness as well as a creaminess to a chunky mix of ice and frozen berries.

When they begin to brown, they get sweeter and let off that banana-y scent. This is when a whole other world opens up. Baked goods need a good brown banana for concentrated caramelized flavor and sweetness.

When you see those boat-like shapes shriveling into a pool of black, syrupy mush (maybe you've just returned from a long weekend?), don't throw them out. Slice open the skin and scoop the flesh into a resealable plastic bag, then label, date, and freeze it. That little pouch of sweetness gets defrosted and whisked into pancake batter or the soaking liquid for French toast. It also adds a full flavor base for any savory-sweet stew such as Indian curry.

bananas flambé with coconut sorbet

serves 4

Bananas are beloved in our household, and eaten for breakfast (page 83), lunch (peanut butter and sliced banana sandwiches), soccer snack (potassium replacement), and this dessert. The simple technique simply simmers the bananas in butter and sugar, which are transformed into a deep rich flavor once the rum hits the pan.

3 tablespoons unsalted butter

¼ cup sugar

2 bananas, sliced on the bias into ½-inch-thick slices

¼ cup rum (I prefer Appleton's Jamaican)

1 pint coconut sorbet or ice cream

⅓ cup unsweetened coconut, toasted

Juice of 1 lime

1 Melt the butter in a large sauté pan over high heat. Sprinkle the sugar evenly over the butter and scatter the banana slices over the sugar in a single layer. Allow the mixture to boil vigorously, undisturbed, until the sugar has melted and the bananas caramelize on the bottom.

2 Remove the pan from the heat and pour the rum into the pan. Carefully ignite the rum in the pan, standing back to avoid the flaring flame. Allow the flame to burn out, about 30 seconds.

3 Divide the bananas and sorbet among four bowls. Top with the toasted coconut and a squeeze of lime juice and serve immediately.

WORTH KNOWING

HOW TO FLAMBÉ

If you're not used to it (or even if you are), torching alcohol in a hot pan can be scary. I have flambéed dozens of times in my life, but once on live television, I didn't realize that my measuring cup of vermouth was too full, and when I dumped it into the pan, it bubbled over onto the gas flame and exploded in a small fire, burning my eyelashes. The flame will always burn out in a short time, so try not to panic if you feel your efforts have gotten a little out of hand. But to ensure that never happens again, I always remove the pan from the stovetop, away from the flame, before adding alcohol, and suggest you do the same.

buttery spiced poached pears

serves 4

When apples and pears are in season from autumn into winter, I keep a large bowl on the countertop for out-of-hand eating. I also love to poach them to transform them into this luscious dessert.

1 cup apple cider

2 tablespoons dry vermouth or dry white wine

2 tablespoons unsalted butter

2 star anise pods or cinnamon sticks

¼ teaspoon coarse salt

3 Anjou or Bartlett pears, peeled, cored, and sliced into 6 slices each

½ cup plain Greek yogurt

2 tablespoons honey

Crisp cookies, for serving (optional)

1 Combine the apple cider, vermouth, butter, star anise, and salt in a large skillet with a tight-fitting lid. Bring to a simmer over medium-high heat. Add the pears, reduce the heat, and simmer, covered, until the pears are tender when pierced with the tip of a knife, 8 to 10 minutes.

2 Whisk together the yogurt and honey. Divide the pears and poaching liquid among four bowls and serve topped with a dollop of honey-yogurt and the cookies, if desired.

chocolate hazelnut orange potstickers

serves 4

Now that wonton skins (also called wrappers) are available in so many big grocery stores, we have another freezer sleeper hit at dessert time. These little bundles, filled with chocolate-hazelnut spread and sprinkled with orange sugar, will melt in your mouth.

1 tablespoon finely grated orange zest (from 1 orange)

½ cup sugar

16 wonton skins (thawed, if frozen)

1 cup chocolate-hazelnut spread, such as Nutella

2 tablespoons unsalted butter

¼ cup water

Vanilla ice cream, for serving

Peeled and separated segments from 1 orange (optional)

1 Combine the orange zest and sugar and set aside. Lay the wonton skins on a work surface and spoon 1 scant tablespoon of the chocolate-hazelnut spread onto each. Brush the edges with water and then fold the skins to form half-moons or triangles. Press the moistened edges together to seal.

2 Heat a 10-inch sauté pan over medium-high heat. Add the butter and water and let the butter melt. Add the chocolate-filled wontons, cover, and simmer for about 3 minutes. Remove the cover and simmer until the liquid has evaporated. Reduce the heat to medium and cook until the bottoms of the wontons become crisp and golden brown. Use a flat spatula to help release them from the pan. (They may stick at first, then release once they are ready.) Blot any butter with a paper towel. Sprinkle the orange-sugar mixture over the wontons and serve with ice cream and orange segments, if using.

SALTY-SWEET IS WHY WE LIKE IT

Salt and pepper. Everyone knows to keep those two shakers next to each other, 'til death do they part. But please recognize this other power couple: salt and sweet. They work in tandem, neither one too dominant, and both sides gently tugging for attention and activating the palate. When the combination is calculated correctly, it's what makes us long for another bite. This is true whether we are eating a dessert or a main dish. When making a marinade for meat, counter the salt and acidic components with some sugar, honey, or maple syrup.

As satisfying as the salty-sweet duo is in savory dishes, it's especially good in desserts. It's what the salted peanuts are all about in an ice cream sundae, or why the mere words "salted caramel" can send us into salivary overdrive. My ideal late-night snack is toasted rustic white bread, sweet butter, and apricot jam—all with a light sprinkling of crunchy salt. Try it and you will see what I mean!

sticky chocolate spoonfuls

makes 8 to 10 spoonfuls; serves 3 to 4

Sometimes, just a bite of something sweet and chocolaty will do. This two-ingredient dessert pulls together a couple of ingredients that are beautiful in their simplicity: sweetened condensed milk and cocoa powder. Combined and rolled into a truffle-like bonbon, this is a popular Brazilian treat known as *bregadeiro*. For dessert, I like to whip up a batch, scoop out multiple teaspoons, and arrange the spoons on a platter for folks to grab and then slowly lick the chocolate off the spoon for an indulgent yet portion-controlled sweet nibble.

One 14-ounce can sweetened condensed milk

¼ cup unsweetened cocoa powder, sifted

Pinch of salt

Pour the condensed milk into a small saucepan. Sprinkle the cocoa and salt over the top, then whisk it into the milk. Place the pan on medium-high heat and stir constantly until the milk thickens and releases from the bottom of the pan, 5 to 8 minutes. Eat immediately by the spoonful or refrigerate until firm enough to roll into bite-size balls.

giofrankie's double chocolate chip cookies

makes about 60 cookies

Add this drop cookie (a specialty of a beloved baking colleague) to my other two favorites—Oatmeal Chocolate Chip (from *Mad Hungry: Feeding Men & Boys*), Banana Chocolate Chip (from *Mad Hungry Cravings*)—and you have a trio of simple, go-to chocolate chip cookies to satisfy anyone. Once cooled, these cookies make excellent ice cream sandwiches. Place a scoop of vanilla ice cream between two of them, press together, wrap in plastic wrap, and freeze.

2¼ cups all-purpose flour, plus more for dusting

1 cup unsweetened cocoa powder

2 teaspoons baking soda

1 teaspoon coarse salt

1¼ cups (2½ sticks) unsalted butter, at room temperature

1¼ cups granulated sugar

¾ cup packed light brown sugar

2 large eggs

1½ teaspoons pure vanilla extract

12 ounces chocolate chips

1. Preheat the oven to 350°F. Line two baking sheets with parchment paper or silicone pads. Whisk together the flour, cocoa powder, baking soda, and salt in a large bowl.

2. In the bowl of a stand mixer fitted with the paddle attachment or using a hand mixer, cream together the butter and sugars until light and fluffy. Add the eggs and vanilla extract and beat well, scraping down the sides of the bowl as needed. On low speed, add the flour mixture, mixing until just combined. Fold in the chocolate chips.

3. Form 1¼-inch balls of dough and arrange them on the lined baking sheets. Bake, rotating the baking sheets and switching the racks halfway through, until the cookies darken around the edges, about 11 minutes. Let cool on the baking sheets for 5 to 10 minutes before transferring to wire racks to cool completely.

EPILOGUE: THE BOYS' STORY

If your parents raise you to believe a certain thing, you are going to have that in your head as being part of your childhood (whether you actually believe it or not). Later on, when you grow up, it's still there because it was a ritual. If parents raise the kid so that every single day he watches them cook and eat healthy food—using vegetables, too—it ultimately has an effect on the kid. It not only balances your life, but your lifestyle. Having that from a young age had a huge effect on me.

—Luca (youngest son)

I can tell you that any kid who has an occupational problem, or problems with attention deficit—you know, just anything that would make a small kid drift off, and get into trouble that they shouldn't be getting in—they need structure from an early age, and food is really good for that. If you can get that kid to shuck corn for an hour, that's an hour that kid is shucking corn and not wandering off and doing something naughty. Try to include even the smallest kid in the prep of food. There is a job for everyone. If potatoes need to be peeled, give him a potato peeler and let him peel potatoes. That's a kind of therapy. For someone with that sort of mind-set, that kind of touching—physically touching food—is very therapeutic, because it calms you down and makes you think about the texture of the potato. It's beautiful—to me it is, anyway.

—Miles (middle son)

Just coming in the kitchen and putting my arm around you and looking at what you were doing. . . . It was spinach, pasta, tomato sauce, with the spinach sautéed in garlic. Garlic started the tomato sauce, garlic started the spinach. That is something I will love for the rest of my life: spinach sautéed in garlic and oil. Sitting in the kitchen just watching you sauté garlic. Garlic in hot oil—that smell, not burned garlic, that smell—garlic sautéing in oil for whatever was going to happen. It's that smell, while just standing behind you and looking around your back, peeking over your shoulder. And that makes me feel happy.

—Calder (eldest son)

For my three sons,
Calder Cory, Miles David, and Luca John

ENTERING THE KINGDOM

As the boy's bones lengthened
and his head and heart enlarged,
his mother one day failed

to see herself in him.
He was a man then, radiating
the innate loneliness of men.

His expression was ever after
beyond her. When near sleep
his features eased towards childhood,

it was brief.
She could only squeeze
his broad shoulder. What could

she teach him
of loss, who now inflicted it
by entering the kingdom

of his own will?
—Mary Karr

ACKNOWLEDGMENTS

Thank you to my whole extended family, near and far, for generation upon generation, as I have always known a safe haven and had a shoulder to lean on and a meal to eat. This book seeks to pay that good fortune forward to all the folks who lay eyes upon it.

If it takes a village to raise a family, then it has taken a small city to wrest the writer out of this cook. Esteemed editor Ann Bramson was the first to say yes to publishing books about our mad hungry madness, and has patiently excavated the relevant know-how from my personal story for three straight books. Under her guidance, a group of gifted editors have all contributed their own particular panache to these pages: Rory Evans, Mary Goodbody, and especially the bright young talent Bridget Monroe Itkin (in for the long haul!).

The graphic design in this and the previous Mad Hungry books has always made me proud, thanks to the skills of Nick Caruso, Jennifer S. Muller, Jan Derevjanik, and Renata Di Biase, led by Michelle Ishay-Cohen. Thank you to Nancy Murray for shepherding the art on these pages to press. Also from the Artisan/Workman team, I am grateful for the contributions of David Schiller, Zach Greenwald, Lelia Mander, and Anna Winslow. Publisher Lia Ronnen, with her forward-thinking and razor-sharp essence, leads her team with a kindness and conviction that I'm completely indebted to.

Photographer Jonathan Lovekin slipped seamlessly into our mad hungry home, with a picture-taking style that has grace, ease, and humor. The same beautiful light he finds in his images lives inside his soul. Tanya Graff contributed an effortless, simple style with her usual confidence.

Food pictures sing when a kitchen team is on point. Michelli Knauer, my soul sister, managed the mayhem with peerless professionalism, with help from Calder and Miles Quinn.

Carla Glasser, loyal agent and friend, has lent her unwavering support and belief to me since before she ever convinced anyone to set my words in print.

My professional career has been enhanced by an A-plus work family of cooks, editors, writers, art directors, designers, stylists, and photographers, which has amounted to an extended graduate school education. Every single one of you has left a mark on my work, for which I am mad obliged.

INDEX